The Sewing Machine Book

also of interest

Short Cut to Fashion: make your own clothes without buying patterns
Sew Simple: a step-by-step guide to dressmaking

The Sewing Machine Book

Myra Coles

Hutchinson
London Melbourne Sydney Auckland Johannesburg

Hutchinson and Co. (Publishers) Ltd
An imprint of the Hutchinson Publishing Group
17–21 Conway Street, London W1P 6JD

Hutchinson Publishing Group (Australia) Pty Ltd
16–22 Church Street, Hawthorn, Melbourne, Victoria 3122

Hutchinson Group (NZ) Ltd
32–34 View Road, PO Box 40-086, Glenfield, Auckland 10

Hutchinson Group (SA) (Pty) Ltd
PO Box 337, Bergvlei 2012, South Africa

First published 1985

© Myra Coles 1985

Designed by Janet McCallum

Cover illustration by Industrial Art Studio

Set in VIP Avant Garde Book by
D. P. Media Limited, Hitchin, Hertfordshire

Printed and bound in Great Britain by
Anchor Brendon Ltd, Tiptree, Essex

British Library Cataloguing in Publication Data
Coles, Myra
  The sewing machine book.
  1. Sewing machines – Amateurs' manuals
  I. Title
  646.2'044   TJ1515

ISBN 0 09 161611 5

Contents

Foreword	7
Preface	9
Acknowledgements	10
1 **Making your choice**	11
2 **Getting to know your sewing machine**	16
3 **Utility stitches**	21
4 **Buttonholes and zippers**	28
5 **Embroidery stitches**	31
6 **Needles, threads and fabrics**	35
7 **Problems**	41
8 **Overlockers**	43
9 **Computer sewing**	51
10 **From witchcraft to wizardry!**	62
Glossary	64
Index	79

Magical movement of needle and thread,
Adventurous rhythms as the fabric is fed,
Creating designs with such intricate ease,
Hither and thither – just where you please:
Intertwining geometrics and scrollwork and line
Never ceasing or resting in creation sublime –
Electrical marvel ahead of your time.

Computerized sewing unique in your style,
Remembering, repeating for mile after mile,
A genius, a genie, mystique of our days,
Flamboyant and gorgeous in so many ways –
Tantalizing electron – you'll always amaze!

Foreword

The great technological advances of recent years have changed our lives in many ways. Not least, they have greatly increased the sophistication of the once-humble sewing machine. For the dressmaker who taps its full potential, it can now open up a new world of fashion possibilities.

We at Vogue Pattern Service know well that there are many dressmakers at all levels of expertise who are keen to take and use all that their sewing machine has to offer. To do this it is not necessary to be a professional oneself; but one requires the guidance of a professional.

So, when we planned a series of articles in Vogue Pattern Magazine to be called 'Mastering your Sewing Machine', we could think of nobody better qualified to write them than Myra Coles, with her expert knowledge, gained over many years, of both sewing and sewing machines. The stream of letters we have received from delighted readers has certainly justified our choice.

The articles also showed Myra that there was scope for a book into which she could assemble the information and advice offered in the articles, plus much more. And here it is.

The author's objective, in her own words, was to produce 'a working manual for sewing machines: to help the beginner, advise the more advanced and stimulate the proficient user'. She has achieved her objective.

Mike Haynes
Managing Director
Vogue Patterns UK

Preface

This is going to be a *positive guide* to help you to master your sewing machine: to give guidance and help on how to get professional results.

Many articles and handbooks are slightly negative, listing all the faults and then what to look for to correct them. I will take the realistic attitude that if you do all the right things then you will, hopefully, not get the problems at all!

There is an amazing amount of information within these pages but it would be an impossibly large book that dealt in minute detail with every single stitch, technique and foot available to the modern sewing machine user – be it she or he! (Lots of men sew too: clothes, sails, camping gear and sports equipment to mention a fraction of what our menfolk are prepared to tackle!)

Over the years I have had the privilege of chatting to machinists all over the UK and I have learned that many problems are universal, some techniques baffling without detailed explanation, and manufacturers' handbooks are technically correct but somewhat narrow in vision: many stitches and techniques have more uses than those recommended in 'the book'. This is hopefully where I take over – to lead you on to experiment where your instruction manual leaves off – or maybe to explain a problem area in slightly more detail.

In no way will you find this a 'dressmaking' book although obviously all that is outlined here will have an influence on your dressmaking and help to give the professional finish that all home dressmakers strive for.

Those of you interested in crafts of various kinds expect different things from your machine – more decoration, more scope with utility stitches, more strength from your stitches and the ability to tackle leather, fur fabrics, canvas, etc.

Whilst the dedicated dressmakers and craftworkers rarely leave their machines for even a day there are millions of people who only take out the machine on a rare occasion, perhaps to make curtains, alter a ready-to-wear garment, mend or patch or maybe make a simple skirt or child's dress.

Whatever your sewing expertise, it is most essential that you are firm friends with your machine and that you know how it will respond in all sewing circumstances. Until your machine is an extension of your own fingers and working 'as one' with you it is impossible to get the very best from it.

It is important too, to recognize the value of machine sewing as a craft in its own right. Hand sewing is *not* better than machine sewing – it is a different technique. Hand embroidery is *not* better than machine embroidery – it is a different technique. There is a place for both crafts in home sewing and I urge sewing machinists to stand up and be counted – to be really proud of the exquisite work produced and not to view machine sewing as second best – *it isn't!*

Myra Coles

Acknowledgements

My very sincere thanks to the following for their help and cooperation in this project:

Especially to Syd Rayner – and the New Home Sewing Machine Company; to Tim le Voi – and Janet Metherell and John Viles at Frister Rossman Sewing Machine Company; and to Pfaff UK and Jones & Brother for permission to reproduce details of their computer machines.

To Vogue Patterns – especially Mike Haynes for his encouragement and to Wendy Rawlins upon whose initial idea the book is based.

To Tootal Sewing Products who generously provided haberdashery and threads for many samples.

Chapter 1
Making your choice

Try to have a positive attitude right from the beginning when you are selecting your machine. Like a car, you must like the look of it, feel at home with the controls (foot pedal, knobs, levers) and know it contains all the stitches and techniques for your type of sewing. If there is even *one* thing that you do not like, or feel uneasy about using – then *do not* buy it: that one little thing will bug you all the years you use the machine and outweigh all the advantages there might be.

I am often asked by ladies contemplating the purchase of a new machine: 'Will I get better results if I pay a little more?' The answer is always: 'Yes, absolutely!' A cheap machine will sew an adequate seam, a more expensive machine will sew a good seam, a top-class machine will sew a perfect seam. Do not expect £700 performance from a £70 machine! However, most discerning dressmakers will find a good machine in the medium-price bracket.

Machines fall into two 'types' within manufacturers' ranges:

Flat-bed machines (Figure 1) will do limited sewing (i.e. straight stitch and zig-zag) at the bottom end of the price range. As prices increase so does the range of stitches and techniques. Flat-bed machines are the traditional type to fit into a sewing cabinet and are often (but not exclusively) heavy in weight.

Figure 1 *Example of a basic flat-bed machine, semi-automatic*

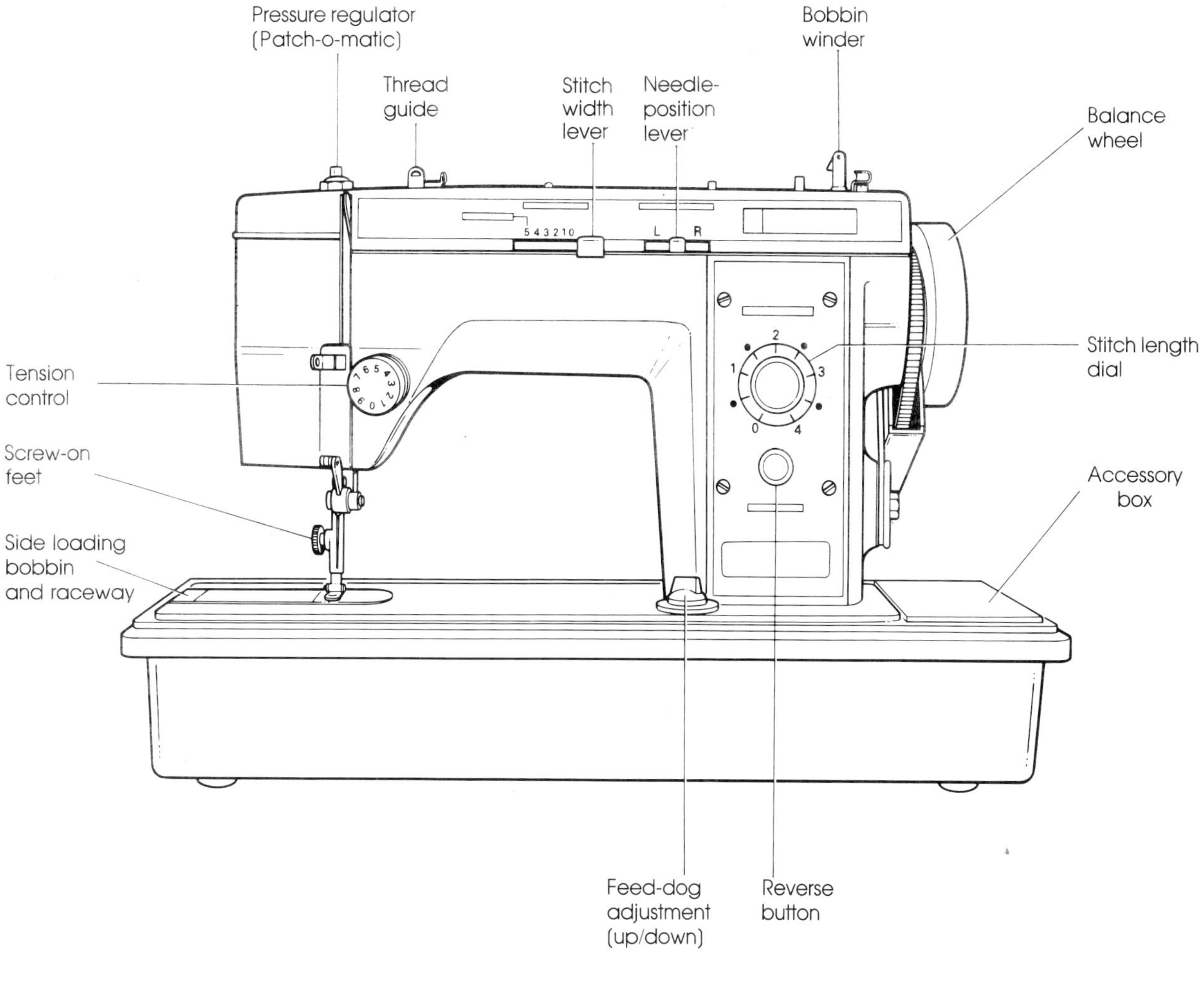

Free-arm machines (Figure 2) (often called sleeve-arm machines). The majority of modern machines incorporate the free-arm which is such a marvellous boon to the dressmaker: the slim arm under the needle makes sewing collars, cuffs, trousers, armholes, sleeves, children's clothes and curved seams so very much easier. The sewing area of a free-arm machine can always be made larger, either by attaching a separate extension plate or by adjusting a movable base-plate incorporated in the machine design.

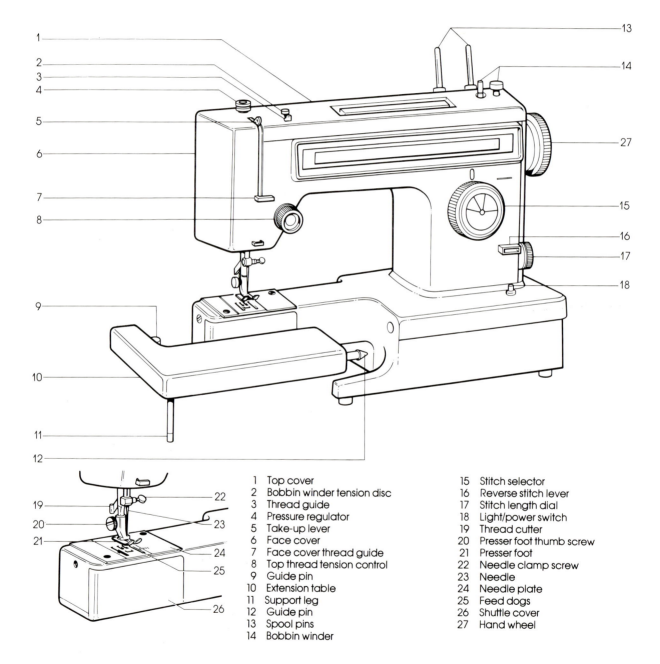

Figure 2 *Example of a mid-range free-arm machine with automatic stitch section*

1 Top cover
2 Bobbin winder tension disc
3 Thread guide
4 Pressure regulator
5 Take-up lever
6 Face cover
7 Face cover thread guide
8 Top thread tension control
9 Guide pin
10 Extension table
11 Support leg
12 Guide pin
13 Spool pins
14 Bobbin winder
15 Stitch selector
16 Reverse stitch lever
17 Stitch length dial
18 Light/power switch
19 Thread cutter
20 Presser foot thumb screw
21 Presser foot
22 Needle clamp screw
23 Needle
24 Needle plate
25 Feed dogs
26 Shuttle cover
27 Hand wheel

Fortunately most manufacturers' ranges also divide reasonably neatly into categories which give an indication of stitches, techniques, quality of performance and, of course, price. The more functions a machine will perform and the smoother the machinery the more expensive you will find it.

Basic machine

Usually this will only do straight stitching and zig-zag.

Semi-automatic (Figure 1)

Usually a reasonably basic zig-zag machine which will provide some extra stitches such as a stretch stitch, blind hem and maybe limited embroidery patterns; sometimes it will include a semi-automatic, four-stage buttonhole.

The machine is set with adjustment of levers/knobs for stitch widths and stitch lengths and often cams are provided separately to produce the individual stitches. The cams are inserted into the body of the machine by the user. This type of machine was extremely popular before the advent of the fully-automatic machine, which now has largely superseded it.

Fully-automatic (Figures 2 and 3)

Quicker and easier to operate than the semi-automatics, these machines have the pattern cams built into the machine and the operator merely selects the stitch required by selector dial. A medium-price machine will include utility stitches and automatic buttonhole; as the price rises so do the stitches and techniques available until perhaps 40 to 50 stitches of utility and embroidery are included. These machines usually do stretch stitches and here the feed dog pushes the fabric forwards *and backwards* as the needle dashes from side to side, putting a reverse-stitch into the seam or embroidery pattern. Embroidery patterns including the reverse stitch will s-t-r-e-t-c-h and so are ideal for embellishing stretch fabrics. Other features to look for in this type of machine are:

1. Variable needle positions;
2. Extra-wide zig-zag sewing: 6–7 mm;
3. Two-stage buttonholes;
4. Basting and tacking facility;
5. De-clutch bobbin winding;
6. Full rotary hook;
7. Snap/clip-on feet.

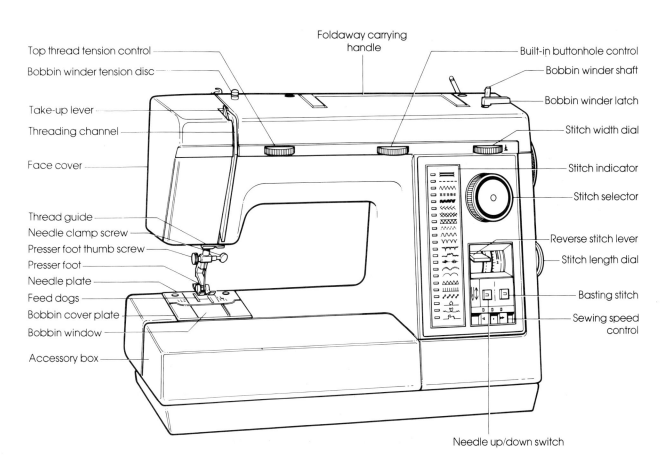

Figure 3 *Example of a fully-automatic machine with electronic features*

Electronic (Figure 3)

These are *mechanical* machines with *electronic* features and must not be confused with *computer* machines.

The electronic features are usually listed by the manufacturer, e.g. electronic foot control; electronic needle penetration; or pattern selection where there is LED (see Glossary) indication of the patterns chosen.

Computer (Figure 4)

Microchip technology has restyled the machine and it has far less moving parts. All stitch selection, programming, buttonhole memorizing, etc. is done by computer. These machines are described in detail in Chapter 9.

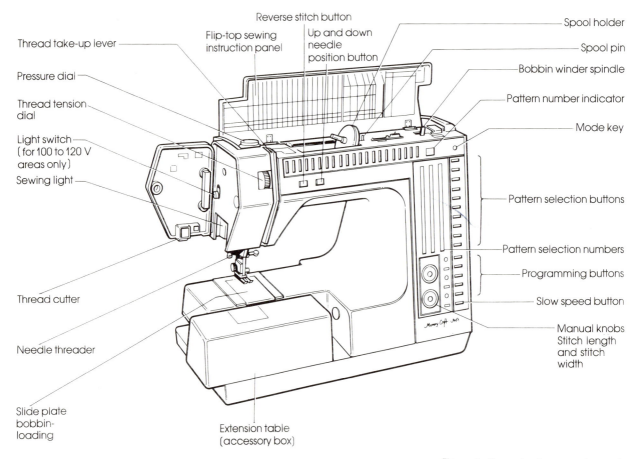

Figure 4 *Example of a computer sewing machine*

Table 1 lists some features and stitches to look out for when buying a new sewing machine. Before you go to a store, list the things you want the machine to do or the type of things you want to sew: it is so easy to forget an important detail when you are faced with a range of twenty or more machines and a very chatty sales person.

When you buy your machine take along some test pieces of fabric of the main types that you use and ask to use the machine yourself; do not just watch the demonstrator. Feel the control that the foot pedal has over the machine, test both the highest speed and the slow-stitch-by-stitch-control which you will also require. Make sure you can easily move the knobs and levers and that you can understand what function they all perform. My *test* for a machine is to do satin stitch. If a machine does a really even satin stitch (buttonhole stitch) it should do all its other functions well too!

Table 1

	Buying your machine	
	What the sewing machine needs to do	*What the sewing machine needs to have*
1	Simple skirts, tops, curtains, alterations, mending	Straight stitch; zig-zag; tricot zig-zag is an advantage. Clearly defined and easy to use controls. Light over the needle
2	A lot of heavy work, household items, upholstery, some toy-making, tailoring	A *heavy* machine incorporating the above. Set in a sewing cabinet if you cannot move it easily but remember a lightweight machine in a cabinet will not have the same results
3	Straightforward dressmaking in a variety of fabrics, children's clothes	A free-arm machine; various needle positions; straight stitch; zig-zag; tricot; straight stretch stitch; *automatic* buttonhole; adjustable pressure on the presser foot; a good assortment of feet; colour-coded controls can be helpful
4	As 3 above plus a lot of fine work/fabrics, more advanced dressmaking and a wide selection of fabrics	As 3 above but with a wider variety of stitches. Even if you do not use all the stitches you will have a machine that gives a better finish on the basic techniques. Also look out for 'outline' zig-zag for bulked fibres such as plushes and stretch towelling; overlocking; stretch overlocking; 7-mm needle swing (amazingly useful); feather stitching (very useful apart from looking pretty); basting; twin needle; snap-on feet; de-clutch bobbin winding
5	Super, top-quality garments for yourself and family with an individual touch, stylish accessories and/or craft items for the home. Ability to tackle *all* fabrics successfully	You will certainly need all the things listed in 4. Invest in a really top-class machine that does 'everything'! Consider a computerized machine which will give you even more scope because you can program it for your own design interpretations and it is so very quick and easy to use. So – you will not use *all* the stitches available every time you sew, but you don't use all the programmes on your washing machine at once do you? It is wonderful to have everything you need built in for the occasions when you *do* need it
6	'Free' embroidery	All machines will do free embroidery, even elderly straight-stitch models
7	'I am a beginner – but I want the simplest machine possible!'	If you can afford it then go for the computerized machine too! It really is the simplest machine to use because it does the thinking for you and takes all the worry out of having to set the dials for various stitch lengths and widths. If you cannot afford the computer machine then have a good *colour-coded system*

Chapter 2
Getting to know your sewing machine

There is so much you can do to get a really professional finish to your garments. The modern sewing machine incorporates an amazing number of stitches and techniques to enable the modern dressmaker to do perfect seams, neatening, zip insertion, buttonholes, top stitching and the 1001 little touches to lift a garment from being just 'very nice' to having the couture touch.

First of all – *don't be afraid of it!* A lot of *ladies* (not so often the men) are nervous of electrical appliances or technical machinery so it is most important to get a good relationship going with your machine. You must really get to know it as well as you know yourself – know every knob, switch, dial: know every setting for every stitch: know its little foibles on various fabrics: know how it will respond to each manoeuvre that you will set in motion.

There is only one way to get to know all this and that is to practise. Practice can be *fun*, so try to make this indispensable time a period of adventure rather than one of boredom. The more experimenting you do the more ideas come along and when you are getting ideas thick and fast you are enthusiastic to try more and more experimenting – it is an endless circle. It can also be fun to share ideas with friends who also like to sew and you will find you all stimulate each other into new experiments. Try a coffee morning now and again to compare projects and encourage each other to try a new technique!

There are some progressive steps to tread along the path of getting to know your machine and also some important dos and don'ts.

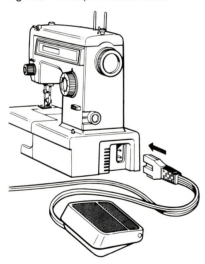

Figure 5 *A foot-pedal attachment*

Step one

If it is to become a true mechanical needle – an extension of your own hands – the first thing to do is to master the control you have over it. Without threading the machine set it up ready to sew: plug it in to the mains, switch it on and attach the foot pedal. Now keep stopping and starting with your foot. Learn just how hard you need to press the pedal to get *instant* needle movement. If you hear a buzzing noise then you need to push your foot down just a little harder: it is similar to taking up the gears in your car – you need to find the *exact* spot. When you have mastered this then experiment with the speed of the machine – just play around and get the feel of it. See Figures 5 and 6.

Step two

If it is a brand-new machine get out your instruction book and learn how to thread machine and bobbin. Thread up over and over again until you are quite conversant with the route of the thread. It is *most important* to go correctly through the tension unit, so pay particular attention here: if you miss going between the little 'silver discs' you will have no tension and the machine will not sew. Figure 7 illustrates a conventional threading system but please note that thread guides do vary from model to model. The format, however, is always the same: the thread passes from the reel (1) – to the tension (2) – to the take-up lever (3) – to the needle (4) – passing through

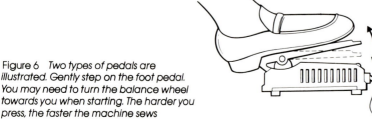
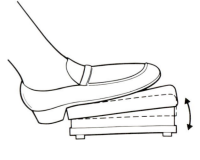

Figure 6 *Two types of pedals are illustrated. Gently step on the foot pedal. You may need to turn the balance wheel towards you when starting. The harder you press, the faster the machine sews*

Getting to know your sewing machine 17

various thread guides en route. Figure 9 illustrates the newest 'easy-thread' system. The tension discs are hidden *inside* the machine between points 2 and 3. You should also have the same thread on the machine and in the bobbin at this stage of your learning session. Use a super-bright colour for practising.

Figure 7 *Threading the top thread. Raise presser-foot lever. Raise the take-up lever to its highest position by turning the hand wheel. Guide the thread through the threading points as shown*

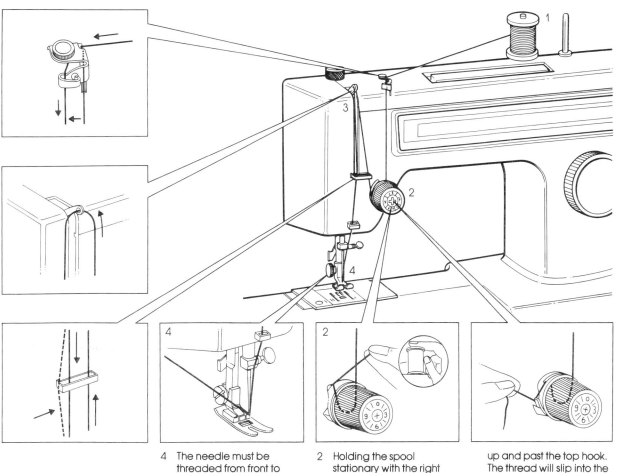

4 The needle must be threaded from front to rear.

2 Holding the spool stationary with the right hand pull the end of the thread between the tension discs. Pull the end of the thread taut so the spring wire loop passes

up and past the top hook. The thread will slip into the hook. Release the thread and the spring wire loop will return to position with the thread as shown.

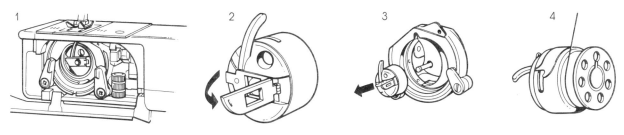

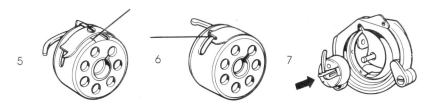

Figure 8 *Example of a bobbin fitting into a bobbin case. Raise the needle to its highest position. Open the shuttle cover and remove the bobbin case from the shuttle by gripping the spring-loaded latch. Insert a full bobbin into the bobbin case as shown. Pull the thread under the tension spring. Holding the latch, position the case into the shuttle, release the latch*
Note: When pulled the thread should turn the bobbin, in a clockwise direction.

Figure 9 Threading the machine. An example of an easy-thread system favoured by most manufacturers for fully-automatic machines. Raise the thread take-up lever to its highest position by turning the balance wheel towards you and guide the thread in the order of 1 to 7

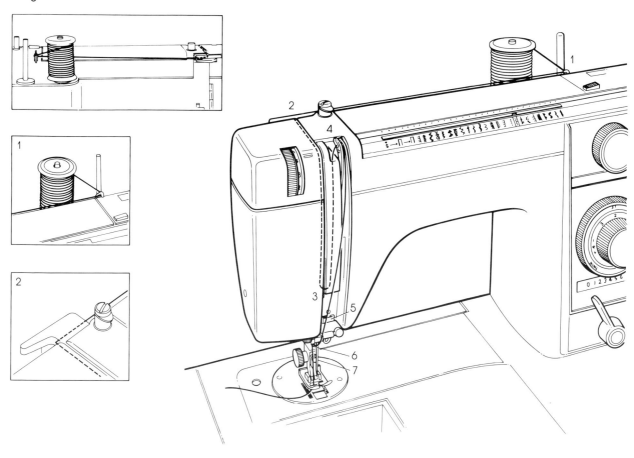

Figure 10 Threading a drop-in bobbin
1 Raise the needle to its highest position
2 Insert the bobbin into the bobbin case, making sure the bobbin rotates in the right direction
3 Pull the thread through slot A and then to the left
4 Pull the thread through slot B and leave about 15 cm of thread

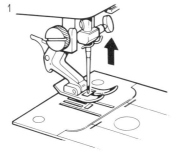
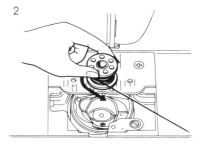
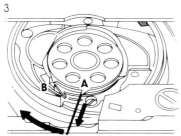
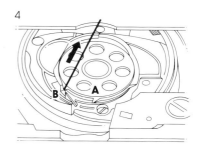

Step three

Get a firm piece of cloth – an old piece of sheeting is ideal – and with fabric *double* start with a straight stitch and sew up and down on various stitch lengths to see how the machine responds. Next programme the basic zig-zag stitch and again sew up and down on various stitch lengths and widths. There are many permutations of lengths and widths and it is interesting just to see what you produce (Figure 11). Gradually work through all the stitches in the same way. Using the instruction book, set the width and length as recommended: when you have seen how the stitch *should* be then alter the length and width to see alternatives – you will be amazed at the different variations produced from a single stitch in this way. For example, a feather stitch on the width of '7' will look incredibly different from a feather stitch on the width of '3'. When you have worked through all the stitches in this way delve into your bit-bag (every dressmaker has a bag of off-cuts!) and try them all again on a variety of fabrics. You will find that on some fabrics they look very different and this will illustrate clearly to you the reasons why some stitches are better on some fabrics – or more suitable – than others. Also it will show you how you can get a variety of special effects on different fabrics.

Be aware of these differences on various fabrics – do not reach for the tension disc because the stitch is 'wrong' – it isn't – it just reacts differently.

It is only in experimenting and playing in this way that you will become confident and familiar with the scope of your stitches. It is a most important – and can be an enjoyable – sewing session. Having familiarized yourself with all the alternatives, when you come to do the stitches on a garment you will know exactly what to expect from each stitch and how to programme your machine for the stitch/effect you require.

When you have another hour or so to spare I would suggest that you do a similar exercise with all the various feet and any other accessories that fit your machine. Again, you will be amazed at what you achieve with this type of relaxed practice session. See Figure 12.

Figure 11 *Examples of stitch length and width controls. Some machines have dials, some have levers. Whatever the system the end product is always the same*

Stitch length is the 'length' of a straight stitch as the machine sews towards you. It is also the 'density' of a zig-zag stitch or embroidery pattern. The lower the number the closer the zig-zag

Stitch width is the 'width' of the side-to-side swing of the needle. '0' will always give a straight line. '1' a tiny zig-zag and thus the higher the number the wider the stitch

Stitch length and stitch width
ST
4
3
2
L
M
0
R
DOWN
TWIN
Stitch length adjust dial
0 1 2 3 4 5 6 7
Stitch width adjust lever

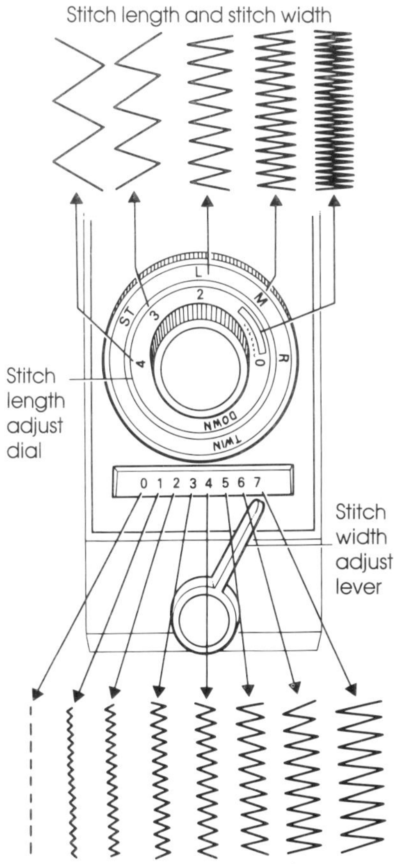

Figure 12 *To achieve optimum sewing results, use the foot recommended by the manufacturer for each sewing technique. Presser feet and their uses are detailed in the Glossary*

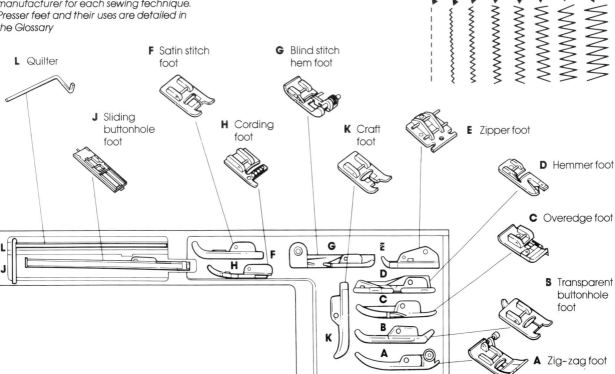

L Quilter
F Satin stitch foot
G Blind stitch hem foot
J Sliding buttonhole foot
H Cording foot
K Craft foot
E Zipper foot
D Hemmer foot
C Overedge foot
B Transparent buttonhole foot
A Zig-zag foot
L
J
F
H
G
E
D
C
B
A
K

Now, some technical dos and don'ts to ensure that your sewing will be trouble-free:

- **Do** Have your machine on a firm table at a comfortable height – *not* balanced on the coffee table!

- **Do** Have a comfortable and stable chair.

- **Do** Have adequate lighting.

- **Do** Keep your machine spotlessly clean and free from dust and fluff. A build-up of fluff around the bobbin area will eventually stop the machine from sewing altogether!

- **Do** Thread the machine slowly and carefully – if you mis-thread the machine it will not sew at all, probably just producing extended loops on the underside of the fabric or snapping the top thread.

- **Do** Make sure your needle is inserted the correct way around. If the needle is inserted back to front the machine cannot sew.

- **Do** Always pull the work out of the machine *backwards* (away from you). This does not strain the needle. It is also important to have the needle at its highest position before taking out your garment – if the machine stops with the needle in the wrong position then turn the balance wheel (*towards you*) to obtain the necessary adjustment. If you do not have the needle at its highest point you will find four threads instead of two pulling up from underneath.

- **Do** Hold on to the two ends of the threads as you start to sew – just until the machine is sewing smoothly. It is not uncommon to get a tangled mess of thread at the beginning of a seam, and sometimes the thread will snap when one of the loose ends gets pulled down into the raceway as the motor springs into action. Just holding the threads will overcome this.

- **Do** Enjoy playing with the machine. Sewing need not be a penance – it should be a pleasurable experience and if you really enjoy a good relationship with your machine, it will be!

- **Don't** Twiddle the tension knob, or screw, indiscriminately! A well-set-up machine will sew 90 per cent of your work without adjustment. Looping below the work, cockled seams and buckled oversewing *are not* necessarily symptoms of tension problems – they can be caused by other means as you will learn later on. So please, don't reach for the tension knob for every problem.

- **Don't** Tackle a big venture (that *superb* designer outfit you have been *longing* to start) on your brand-new machine the minute you get it home. Spend a few hours experimenting and when you are familiar with your new stitches and techniques *then* get going on the special project.

Chapter 3
Utility stitches

It is so sad that so many superb sewing machines are not used to their full potential. Sometimes it is because the user is unsure of the mechanical operation of the machine. Another reason for not using the machine to greater effect is being unsure of when to use certain stitches. The manufacturer's instruction booklet provided with the machine usually explains what a certain stitch is for — but from experience we know that most utility stitches can be used very effectively in a surprisingly large number of ways.

Listed are some of the most important, or 'working', stitches found on modern machines. Working stitches are for constructing garments and whilst some can be used for embellishment this is not their primary function. Purely decorative stitches will be found later.

Table 2

Stitch symbol	Stitch	Various uses
ǀ ǀ ǀ	Straight stitch	For seams, darts, top stitching, quilting, gathering and zip insertion
⟨⟩⟨⟩⟨⟩	Zig-zag	For seam neatening, buttonholes and appliqué
⟩⟩⟩	Tricot stitch or 3-step zig-zag	For sewing elastic, for seam neatening (on all types of fabric), for darning and for added strength
⧠	Overlock	A stretch seam and overlocking finish all in one operation — also suitable for handknits and even non-stretch fabrics
⟨ǀ⟨	Blind hem	For a quick and easy hem on skirts, trousers and curtains — also shell tucks and shell edging
ǀǀǀ ǀǀǀ ǀǀǀ	Triple stretch stitch or true stretch stitch	The true stretch stitch for seams, darts, and polo-necks. Excellent for a heavy top stitching line and for inserting zips into denim and other similar heavy-duty sewing
⋝⋝	Feather stitch	A very stretchy stitch suitable for seaming jumpers, and as a decorative stitch, suitable for patchwork and lace appliqué
⧹⧹⧹	Ric-rac	For sewing plush, double-knits, swim-wear, etc. for stretch neatening, strength and decoration

If you do a fair amount of dressmaking you need, and will use, all of these stitches once you get used to them, because for a really professional finish on various fabrics, you do require the flexibility they offer.

Taking these utility stitches in sequence it is interesting to probe into them in depth to understand how and why they can improve your sewing.

Straight stitch

See Figures 13(a), (b), (c) and (d).

Top stitching in straight stitch can be used to great effect for finishing touches.

Figure 13
(a) Piping and top stitching complement each other in a contrast colour to the black velour. Vogue pattern. Garment by Myra

Figure 13 – continued
(b) (c) Two interesting designs showing the use of machined or top-stitched hems. Courtesy Vogue Patterns

(d) Top stitching adds interest to a garment but is also necessary to hold and support various design details. Courtesy Vogue Patterns

Zig-zag

See Figures 14, 15 and 16.

A word about basic zig-zag. Don't reserve it just for overcasting. Any machine that does a zig-zag will do a satisfactory buttonhole. Use that buttonhole stitch, or *satin stitch* as it is known, to do appliqué and corded hems and to apply lace to your lingerie. Use it too to provide a very narrow edging on frills, flounces, collars, scarves etc. instead of a rolled hem: setting '1' wide and '1' long.

When you use this stitch as an edging *never* use it by actually sewing over the edge of the fabric. Place the edge of the lace at least the width of the foot away from the fabric edge. This will prevent buckling and cobbling which can be so very annoying and frustrating. Then trim away excess fabric very closely with sharp scissors.

Figure 14 Applying lace to fabric edge with zig-zag

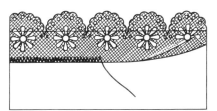

Figure 15 Trimming fabric edge after applying lace

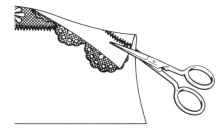

Figure 16 The application of lace is time-consuming but the results are more than rewarding. Vogue and Butterick patterns. Garments by Myra

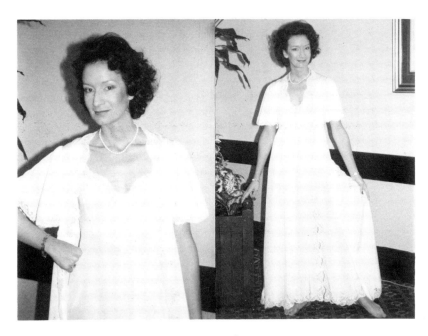

Tricot stitch or three-step zig-zag

See Figures 17 and 18.

Tricot stitch is exactly the right stitch to sew knicker elastic on to underwear and for elasticated cuffs, ankles and waistlines. But this stitch will cope with very much more.

Most sewers use ordinary zig-zag for overcasting raw edges. Have you ever used it on flimsy fabric and found that the edges are all puckered? Three-step zig-zag will triumph here. Use it on a narrow width setting (perhaps '3') and use it either over the edge or *just inside* the edge and you will have a very neat, flat, overcasting. On a tweedy or heavy fabric use it wide — on '7' if possible — and see how well it secures all those stray fibres.

For mums with small children, damaged clothes are commonplace. Small tears, jagged rips and worn-through knees on trousers can all be tidily repaired with three-step zig-zag. Here you need to set the stitch length on a very low number ('1' or '1.5') and run backwards and forwards over the area to be secured. A small piece of lining, Vilene or other thin fabric behind the mend will support the stitches for even greater durability.

Straight stretch stitch

See Figures 19 and 20.

Designed as a stretch stitch and therefore often totally overlooked for other jobs, this is probably the most neglected of the modern stitches. Because this stitch s-t-r-e-t-c-h-e-s it is ideal for firmer jerseys (not the very silky ones!) but since a back stitch is involved in the sequence which produces the stitch it is *very strong* and thus can be used for strength even when the fabric *does not stretch*. It is fantastic for jeans, denim jackets, etc.; amazing for zips in trousers, bags and other places where the strain will be great; ideal for upholstery, sails and other sporting items where great strength is required.

It is also an extremely useful stitch for bold top stitching. A normal polyester thread will show up well, but if you use a bold or buttonhole twist thread it will be positively stunning. Tip here: use the heavy thread on the top of the machine and leave the thinner thread with which you have made the garment on the bobbin.

Figure 16 – continued

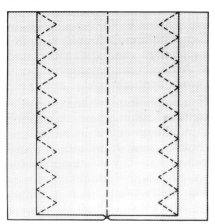

Figure 17 Tricot stitch or three-step zig-zag

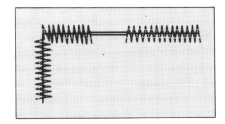

Figure 18 Repairing a tear with three-step zig-zag on a low-number setting

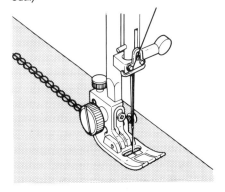

Figure 19 Straight stretch stitch is sewn with two stitches forward and one stitch backward forming a seam that does not rip easily

Figure 20 Bold thread – straight stretch stitch and quilting for shoulder emphasis on velvet. Vogue pattern. Garment by Myra

Figure 21 Feather stitch

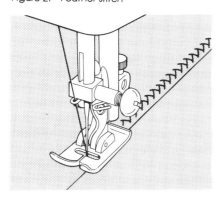

Feather stitch

See Figures 21 and 22.

Feather is now included on many brands of sewing machine. Although it looks like an embroidery stitch (and is of course – we will look at it again later!) it is in fact a very useful working stitch often overlooked.

Two things to note: it incorporates a back stitch so it is strong and also it will stretch.

If you need strength somewhere, but feel that a zig-zag looks rather utilitarian, then feather is the answer because it looks prettier. It is ideal for patchwork and appliqué because it not only looks good, it holds the pieces very firmly.

Because it stretches you can use it on stretch fabrics and thus get good-looking strength and stretch together.

It is excellent for putting real jumper knits together: either a knitted garment you have made by hand or machine or those knitted fabrics that you can buy by the metre. Using this stitch with knitted fabrics enables you to sew the seam and cut off the surplus seam allowance to provide a nicely neatened and stretchy seam. (When using feather stitch, you will find the knitted stitches do not unravel when the fabric is cut.)

Figure 22 Appliqué – the simplest and quickest way to give interest to clothes or crafts. Courtesy Butterick

Overlock

See Figures 23 and 24.

There are many overlock stitches now available on domestic machines but these overlock stitches are different from the commercial type (see Chapter 8).

Figure 24 illustrates four of the overlock stitches widely available on various makes of machine plus zig-zag and tricot stitch which are also used to overcast.

Overlock   A stretchable seam and overcast in one operation. It can also be used successfully on non-stretch fabrics. It can be sewn over the fabric edge or if puckering occurs place the edge of the foot on the fabric edge, sew the seam and then trim the waste fabric afterwards. Use widths from 3 to 7 mm.

Double-edged zig-zag   A super stitch for fabrics that fray a lot – medium wools, tweeds, linen and raw silk. Ideal as a single-thickness overcast but can seam and overcast in one operation. Use widths 3 to 7 mm.

Knit stitch   This is widely used by various manufacturers. Recommended for hand and jumper knits, swimwear and plush fabrics. Seam and overcast in one operation: sew on the seam line and trim excess fabric afterwards. Ideally use width '5', but this is flexible.

Professional overlock   A new stitch on computer machines which looks very like the commercial finish and gives a very professional look to the home dressmaker's work. Can be used as a single over-edge finish or as a seam and overcast in one operation on most fabrics. Use as programmed.

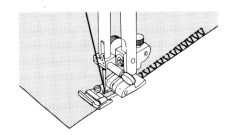

Figure 23   *Overlock stitch on a fabric edge*

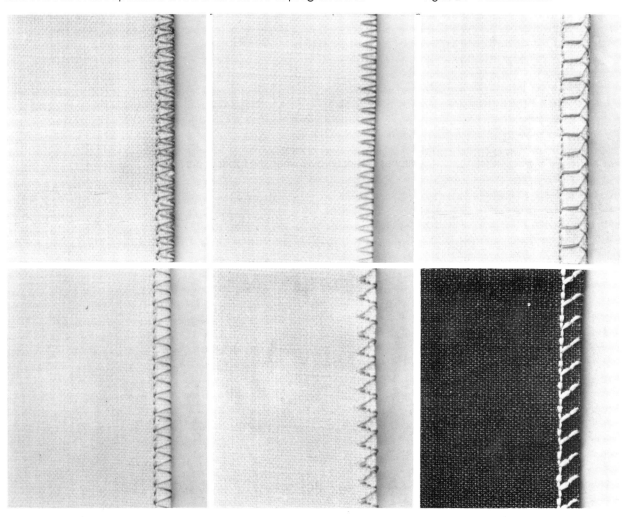

Figure 24   *Overlock stitches*

Figure 25 To set blind stitch hem guide. Loosen the quilter set screw and insert the blind stitch hem guide. Then tighten the screw firmly

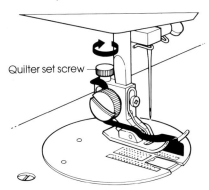

Quilter set screw

Blind hem stitch

See Figures 25, 26, 27 and 28.

Blind hemming An effective finish but it is one not found particularly easy. Use on *straight* skirts, trousers, curtains etc. Do not use on very flared or circular garments. Difficulties are often caused because the fabric is not folded correctly under the presser foot during stitching. Hopefully Figure 25 will help those of you who are confused! On lightweight fabrics the raw edge can be turned under and pressed flat before hemming – but most fabrics respond well to the raw edge being overcast/overlocked and so the hem is much flatter and less obtrusive. The foot illustrated is the latest designed for this technique and used by various manufacturers. Other machines will probably have a small guide supplied which slips into place between the normal presser foot and the large press-foot screw (Figure 26).

Figure 26

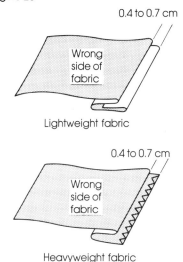
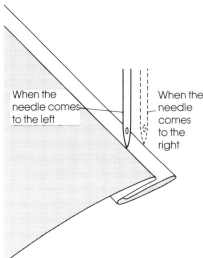
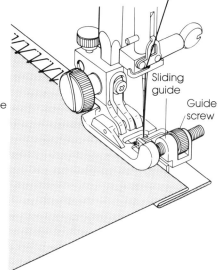

(a) On lightweight fabrics the raw edge can be turned under and pressed. On heavyweight fabrics that ravel, the raw edge should be overcast first. Fold up the desired amount and pin it in place. Then fold the hem under the fabric as shown

(b) Position the fabric so that the needle just pierces the folded part of the fabric when the needle comes over to the left side. Lower the presser foot

(c) Turn the guide screw and move the sliding guide next to the folded edge. Sew, guiding the folded edge along the sliding guide. For a professional-looking hem fold the fabric reducing the lip to a scant 2 mm. As you sew, the right-hand stitch will fall off the fabric edge, forming a chain stitch

Figure 27 Shell tucks

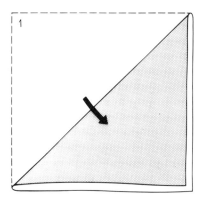
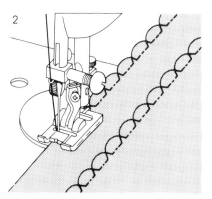
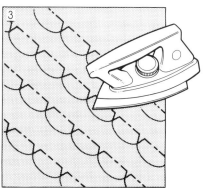

1 Fold the fabric on the bias

2 Place the fabric under the presser foot as shown. Be sure that the needle does not penetrate the fabric at its left needle position

3 Unfold the fabric and press the tucks to one side with an iron

Shell tucks and hems (Figures 27 and 28) Use the blind hem stitch with a tightened top tension. The amount of adjustment will depend on the fabric in use and a test piece must be done on various tension numbers to discover the required effect on a particular cloth.

Make a note of the tension setting before you start ... and as soon as you have completed the tucks re-adjust back to the original setting before you forget!

Fabrics should be folded on the bias for a successful finish, the exception being knits which can be tucked in any direction.

Ric-rac

Ric-rac is the zig-zag equivalent to the straight (or triple) stretch stitch and is both strong and decorative as well as being a stretch stitch. Can be used on widths 3 to 7 mm.

Figure 28 *Completed shell tucks*

When trying out all these various stitches and permutations of widths and lengths it is a considerable help to *write down* your findings. Do a 'sampler' on a piece of firm cloth showing all the stitches and variations. As you go along write the machine settings *on to the cloth* with a felt-tip pen, thus reserving these details for later sewing sessions. It is surprisingly easy to forget! It is also helpful to put the sample work into a folder and add to it over forthcoming sewing sessions.

A small off-cut of fabric from each outfit you make, with some sample stitches that you have used, is really most useful for future reference, too. Also a notebook is handy to jot down any technical points to remember plus, perhaps, washcodes, trimmings used and pattern numbers.

Chapter 4
Buttonholes and zippers

Figure 29 Buttonhole sequence

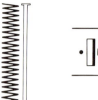
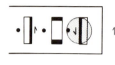

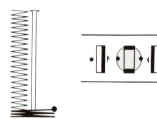

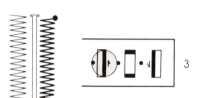

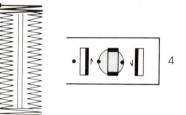

In between utility or working stitches and embroidery come buttonholes and zipper insertion.

Great strides have been made by manufacturers in this area and performing these techniques is now much simpler.

All manufacturers' instruction books will give clear guidance on your machine's capabilities but it could be of interest here to look at some of the most up-to-date systems.

Buttonholes

The 'standard' automatic buttonhole is 'dialled' on the stitch selector in four easy stages.

Mark the length of the buttonhole required (i.e. size of button + 3 mm (⅛ in)), place the fabric under the presser foot and the sequence is as shown in Figure 29:

1 Down the first side
2 Bar tack
3 Up the second side
4 Bar tack

Fully-automatic machines with embroidery can have an even simpler system and a two-step buttonhole is amazingly quick and easy.

Having 'dialled' the buttonhole the machine will bar tack A and sew down one side B and when the required length is reached on a mere touch of the controls the machine will sew the second bar tack C and up the second side (Figure 30).

Some machines provide a specialist foot into which you insert the button to be used and the machine will self adjust and make you a perfectly sized buttonhole each time.

Equally simple are the computer machines which will 'remember' the size of the buttonhole and repeat it time after time.

Remember, whatever your machine:

Figure 30 Fully-automatic buttonhole-making

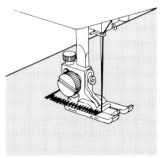

Always! Do a test buttonhole on a spare piece of fabric. *Not* just one layer! — reconstruct your garment in miniature with the same layers of fabric *and interfacing* and on the same grain lines. Failure here can result in a buttonhole too small, too large, or too tightly sewn.

Always! Interface buttonholes — both the samples and those on the garment. This takes the strain of the stitches and the strain of constant use.

Unsure! Start with the bottom buttonhole in the garment and work upwards towards the neckline and the one that will show most in wear.

Cut! With the buttonhole cutter supplied with the machine and not with large scissors. If you place a pin across the bar tack it will save slicing through a larger portion of your garment than intended! See Figure 31.

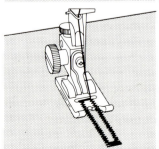

Figure 31 *Place a pin just below the bar tack at each end to prevent accidentally cutting the bar tacks. Cut the opening with the buttonhole cutter*

Buttonholes and zippers 29

For extra strength on a suit, coat, trousers or skirt, try a corded buttonhole (Figure 32). An embroidery or crochet thread can be used and the buttonhole is made in the usual way with the 'cord' aligned under the special buttonhole foot. When the buttonhole is complete pull the left end of the filler cord to tighten: with a darning needle take threads through to the reverse side and cut.

Figure 32 A corded buttonhole

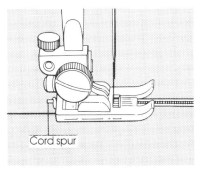
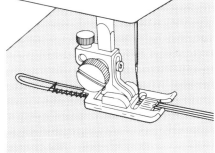
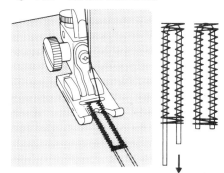

(a) Hook the filler cord over the cord spur of the buttonhole foot from behind

(b) Sew starting with the bar tack. Sew the left row

(c) Sew the other bar tack. Sew the right row and reinforce the stitches. Pull the right or left end of the filler cord to remove slackness. Cut off excess cord

A selection of buttonhole presser feet is available – see the Glossary.

If you need to alter the balance of the stitching this can be done by adjusting the balance guide on your machine. Please refer to your personal manual for placement of the balance guide – an example is shown in Figure 33.

Figure 33 Example of adjustment of buttonholes stitch balance. When you set the adjustment knob, use the same material and thread as those you intend to use for buttonhole stitching

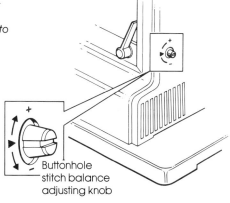
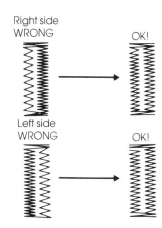

Zippers

Figure 34 Adjusting a zipper foot

The way that you insert your zipper depends on the garment and type of zipper and it is recommended that you refer to your pattern instructions and/or a dressmaking book (e.g. *Vogue Sewing*) for general information on whether to use a concealed, semi-concealed or invisible zipper method.

Whatever you choose here are a few tips for sewing:

1 Ensure the tape is held firmly whilst stitching.
2 Always use the zipper foot. (Various types are illustrated in the Glossary.)

Fit the zipper foot on to the machine and (Figure 34) move the foot by means of the screw at the back (A) into the correct sewing position: the needle should be adjacent to the left or right semi-circular notch (B) in the foot. Use left or right, whichever is most practical.

Some fully automatic machines have a 'fixed' zipper foot and the *needle* is moved into the correct sewing position.

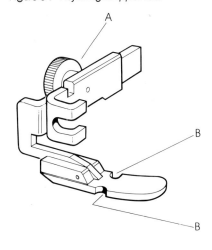

Figure 35 *Invisible zipper insertion*

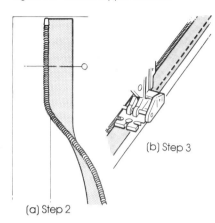

(a) Step 2 (b) Step 3

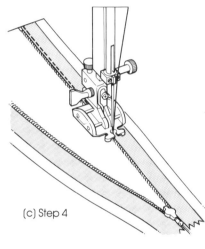

(c) Step 4

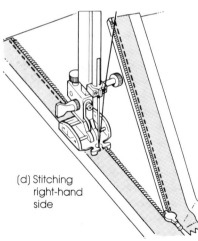

(d) Stitching right-hand side

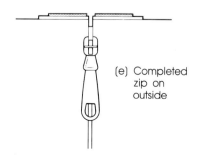

(e) Completed zip on outside

Invisible zippers

Good-quality ready-to-wear garments usually have invisible (or concealed) zippers. These are sadly neglected by the home dressmaker, which is a great pity because they ensure success every time – once you know how to use them.

Invisible zippers are now widely available from the larger department stores but not often in a prominent position! Please note that an *ordinary* zipper cannot be inserted invisibly. The invisible zipper is a specialist item. They are a little more expensive (pennies not pounds!) but really are worth the little extra for the professional finish obtained and ease of insertion.

At least two major sewing machine companies include an invisible zipper foot with their top machines – if one is not included in your kit then purchase one separately – various makes do fit other machines.

This type of zipper is suitable for all fabrics from fine silk crêpe de chine and silky jerseys through to suit-weight wools and tweeds, and can be inserted into skirts, trousers and dresses. Totally invisible on the right side of the garment, the opening merely looks like another seam.

Use the following sequence to insert and *remember* the zipper is laid on the *right side* (outside) of the garment. See Figure 35.

1. Do not sew the seam *below* the zip.
2. Open the zipper and lay the left size on the garment as illustrated – the teeth on the seam line (usually 15 mm (⅝ in) inside the fabric edge) and the top of the zipper opening (approximately 6 mm (¼ in) below the waist/neck seam line). Pin into place with pins at 90 degrees to the zip.
3. With zipper foot or normal presser foot sew the zip into place on the outside edge of the tape.
4. Using the invisible zipper foot sew the stitching line *under* the teeth: needle in the central hole and teeth under the left-hand 'tunnel'.
5. When the foot reaches the zip pull/tag either 'lock-off' or do one or two reverse stitches to fasten off.
6. Repeat steps 2–5 on the right-hand side of the tape and garment, using the right-hand tunnel on the foot.
7. Close zip.
8. Lay out the garment and pin or tack the seam from hemline to zipper.
9. Stitch from the hem upwards towards the zip on the seamline, using the zipper foot with the needle on the right-hand outside of the foot: when you reach the zipper continue sewing alongside the previous stitching line for 1.25–2 cm (½–¾ in) and then lock-off. This overlap is *vital* so that there is not a 'poke' at the bottom of the zip in wear.

Chapter 5
Embroidery stitches

To enable the modern sewing machine to move on from utility stitches to embroidery or 'fancy' stitches takes only the flick of a switch or button. To attune the mind of the seamstress to the acceptance of these stitches can be quite another matter! See Figure 36.

Very often machine embroidery has been slated and derided by expert hand embroiderers, the result being that the machine sewer often has quite a guilt complex about incorporating these stitches into her work – *What a waste! What a disaster!*

It really cannot be emphasized too strongly that hand and machine embroidery are *not* on competitive terms, they are two entirely different art forms and both should stand alone in their own right.

It is also a very sad fact that these stitches may also be neglected for a different reason. 'It's too difficult' – 'I haven't got enough time to fiddle around' are both frequent excuses for not using machine embroidery. These in fact veil the probable real reason, which is usually lack of confidence.

I have described how to have an enjoyable but vitally important practice session with your sewing machine, in order to feel total confidence with and control over it. It is also so important to try the embroidery stitches in the same way and the best method is to test all the stitches on all the width and length settings, as well as those recommended in the instruction book. Start with a firm fabric and then try them on a variety of bits and pieces from the bit-bag to understand how they are formed and how they can be adapted to suit your needs. See Figure 37.

Figure 36 Appliqué, ribbons, lace and smocking. Children like bold designs and clear colours. Vogue and Butterick patterns. Garments by Myra

Figure 37 Learn your own and your machine's capabilities by practising all the embroidery stitches
Illustrations of computer embroidered stitches

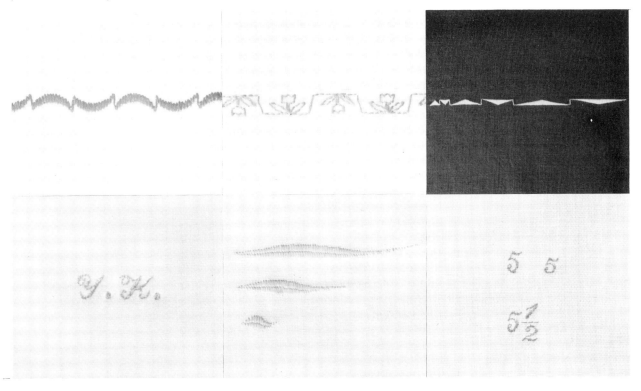

Figure 38 *Satin-stitch machine embroidery*

Figure 39 *Open-stitch machine embroidery*

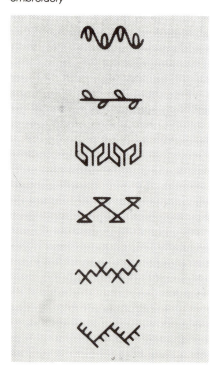

Use normal sewing thread, normal needles and normal feet. Try various threads – Sylko, Gütterman, Coats, Sylko Supreme, bold, buttonhole twist, pure silk, Molnycke. Try them all, but leave the bobbin thread the same (i.e. normal sewing thread). It is interesting to discover how the thickness of the threads becomes quite apparent in the design of the pattern and indeed you will be very surprised at the variety of thicknesses you will find just within the range of threads I have exampled. Satin-stitch patterns will look particularly striking with heavier threads and the open patterns even more spidery with a fine thread. Notice the sheen on the mercerized cottons and the matt effects of some of the polyesters.

Keep an open mind about the results you obtain. In this area of machining nothing is right or wrong! The recommendations in the instruction book will guide you on obtaining the design as illustrated but by altering the width and/or length controls you can obtain your own variations to suit your fabric, designs and own personal taste. Again, when practising and experimenting initially use a firm fabric.

It is no more difficult to do a row of machine embroidery than a row of straight stitches and it takes only a few minutes longer!

It is important, though, to become familiar with your embroidery stitches, choices and capabilities *before* setting out to embroider or embellish any project at all. Make sure you become aware of the two different pattern types briefly mentioned earlier – satin-stitch patterns and open-stitch patterns.

Satin-stitch patterns (see Figure 38) are lovely rich, bold, designs which are programmed with buttonholes in mind.

The width setting can vary from approximately 3– 7 mm but the stitch length must be very close – just like your buttonhole setting. All machines vary, but whatever make you use the length for satin stitching will be around 0.5 to 1.5 depending on the thickness of your thread. If you have the machine set on a longer stitch length such as 3– 4– 5 it will produce quite a meaningless jumble of zig-zag stitches.

Open-stitch patterns (see Figure 39) are beautiful, intricate patterns where the needle dashes from side to side whilst the feed dog is pushing the fabric backwards *and* forwards. Quite a funny sensation until you get used to all this movement.

It is important here to have your stitch length on the *long* setting (or high number). Quite the opposite to the satin stitches. The width setting is variable and usually between 3– 7 mm.

The fabric moving backwards and forwards is putting reverse (or back stitches) into the design. This happens in the simplest form with straight stretch stitch. A reverse stitch always denotes s-t-r-e-t-c-h so it means that these open embroidery stitches with reverse stitches *will stretch* and can be used with great effect and with undoubted success on stretch jerseys of all kinds – even the fine, soft, silky ones.

With the vast range of stitches available do consider some embroidery stitches for *sewing techniques* not just as embellishment. Examples are faggoting, fringing, smocking, quilting, edging, hemming, patchwork and appliqué. See Figure 40.

Deciding to use satin-stitch or open-stitch patterns is often one of personal choice and dependent on the fabric being used but I will detail some specific ideas and uses for embroidery generally. Whole books can be written on this subject so here I intend merely to stimulate your interest with some simple but effective ideas. Hopefully experimentation will lead you down exciting new paths that you never thought you would dare to tread.

- Use a single row of embroidery for top stitching instead of a line of straight stitch. Matching thread to fabric (rather than a contrast) can give an understated elegance.

Figure 40 *Two patchwork craft items by Myra, to her own design. The combination of threads, texture, quilting, colour and intricate stitching gives added dimension to two basically simple ideas*

Don't forget that you will need to purchase two or three extra reels of thread for your garment when using embroidery stitches in this way.

- Use a line of embroidery instead of a straight line when hemming the linings of skirts, jackets and coats. On jackets and coats, too, use an embroidery stitch to hold the pleat of the lining in place at the neck, the waist and hemline. Traditionally this was a hand cross-stitch feature but machine embroidery adapts well. These touches look superb and expensive.

- Use contrasting coloured embroidery to emphasize construction details or seaming and on collars, pockets, yokes and pleats. This is particularly nice on children's and modern casual wear.

- Feature a zip with a line of embroidery either side – particularly good used in conjunction with the chunky zippers now available. Contrast zip and thread to the main fabric shade.

- Quilting with embroidery is just as easy as quilting with straight lines. Luscious for heavy silks, satins or moirés. Add beads afterwards by hand for extra-special effects. Superb on velvet too, if you use satin stitches and bold or buttonhole twist.

- Match lace and thread and alternate rows of lace and embroidery around hems of nightwear, slips or children's dresses.

- Combine appliqué and embroidery for fun designs on tops, jackets, dresses and beachwear. Some extremely brilliant (coloured) machine embroidery threads are available – also gold, silver and lurex.

- Machine smocking is so effective and can be done over rows of hand or machine gathers. *Don't* expect it to look just like hand smocking because it won't! But it is fun and can look really expert if you take care with your colours.

- Patchwork can be given a new dimension. A number of stitches are both suitable and successful but it is recommended to use only one on each piece of work or the results can look rather confusing. The Victorians did beautiful random patchwork with feather stitchery. This idea translates particularly well into the sewing machine with velvets and soft leathers. Butt the pieces together and back with a medium-weight Vilene. Use a bold thread on the top of the machine, finer thread on the bobbin.

Another type of patchwork particularly suitable for the machine is log cabin. The strips of fabric are always sewn with straight stitches so once you have the formula for piecing the strips it is quick and straightforward.

- Embroider on leather! Not as outrageous as it sounds because modern machines cope extremely well with this luxury medium. Leather needles are readily available and their use is recommended although on *very* soft suedes you can often cheat with a scarfed needle to good effect. A roller foot, Teflon, or even-feed foot will help the leather to pass through the machine smoothly, but having selected the suitable foot and needle you need do nothing more than select your stitch and start sewing – the effect is gorgeous. If you are using a medium to heavy leather a buttonhole or bold thread looks good – leave Sylko or similar finer thread on the bobbin.

- Ribbon can be applied in many ways to considerable effect. On jersey or wool suits and dresses made in a plain fabric a velvet or satin ribbon stitched over the seam lines emphasizes them and gives an extremely smart finish: understated again, if you match ribbon and fabric colour although a contrast or toning colour can be chic. Rows of ribbon applied with embroidery stitches give a personalized 'braid' effect. Matching thread colour to ribbon and doing alternate rows of embroidery and applied ribbon on skirts and jackets gives an interesting contrast of textures. Permutations of ribbon and embroidery are endless and it is worth playing around with your own design ideas.

- If you are sewing a picture, design or border with lots of different-coloured threads you need not have lots of different-coloured bobbins too: just *match the bobbin thread to the fabric* and change only the top threads as required.

Chapter 6
Needles, threads and fabrics

Needles

Thankfully some years ago manufacturers decided to make standard-sized needles for all makes of machines – this was a superb step forward and so it is now possible to use a variety of specialist needles retailed by various companies. There are, for example, twin and triple needles, and wing needles (for hem stitching and drawn-thread work) all widely available and interchangeable between makes. If you are using an older machine take your standard needle along to the shop to make comparisons before purchase – and seek the help and advice of the specialist in the sewing machine department of the store. Although needles are available in the haberdashery areas it is the demonstrator/consultant in the sewing machine department who is trained to help and advise. Use their knowledge for this and in fact many other sewing matters.

The most common 'fault' on a new machine usually turns out to be a wrongly inserted needle. This simple rule applies to most machines: if your bobbin goes into the machine from the *side*, the flat part of the needle faces the *right-hand* side of the machine []→: if the bobbin goes into the machine at the *front* (or *behind* the needle) the flat part of the needle faces away from you ↑.

It is most important to replace your needles regularly. Needles go blunt surprisingly quickly, particularly when you are using synthetic fabrics, so be prepared to change your needle after making every garment. Remember too, to *throw it away* when you have taken it out of the machine. *Never* keep it for use at a later date. Ballpoint needles also need to be changed just as often. Blunt needles will not only damage the fibres in your fabric they will also start to skip stitches. You can also skip stitches if your needle is too small or too large for the fabric you are sewing – e.g. an '18' on crêpe de chine or an '11' on denim.

Size '14' needles (continental size '90') were considered average before synthetic fabrics made such an important impact on sewing. This is still a good choice for many medium weights of wool and cottons, but now we tend to consider an '11' ('70') 'average' for modern fabrics. Numbers '16' and '18' ('100' and '120') are for coats and heavyweight sewing tasks. Number '9' ('60') is still available from manufacturers so chivvy your local dealer if he or she does not stock them: these extra-fine needles are invaluable for excessively fine work.

A most interesting but little-known fact, is that *ballpoint needles will work beautifully on all fabrics! Yes*, even 100 per cent cottons, silks and wools. Designed originally for nylons, synthetic fabrics and jerseys they have now become standard for most sewing tasks. Available usually in packets of size '11' ('70') they are also available in mixed-size packets in some cases.

Manufacturers are constantly updating their products and now there is an improved ballpoint called a **scarfed needle**. The difference is a technical one relating to the length of the cut-away part of the shank above the eye. Use it on all fabrics – synthetic or natural – and if not obviously available on your haberdashery shelves again ask the local demonstrator/consultant.

Also quite new is the **Teflon needle**. Yes it is black and looks just like the inside of your frying-pan. Try this for the heavier synthetic jerseys, double-knits and Crimplene-type fabrics, plushes, single knits, knits and PVC.

Jeans needles are a fantastic new development. Extraordinarily strong, they slice through denim just like butter. Do try them too, not only for jeans but upholstery work, repairs on tents, awnings, canvas sails, garden furniture and other heavyweight repair jobs.

Leather needles have a blade rather than a normal point which will slice through leather without damaging the skins. Use normal settings on your machine and a cotton or all-purpose thread for sewing seams. Embroidery on leather is perfectly practicable and in this instance the buttonhole twist can give excellent results (finer thread on the bobbin) but Sylko 40 and even the pure silk threads look marvellous too.

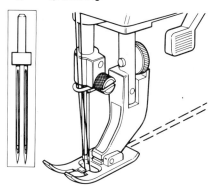

Figure 41 *Twin needles give perfectly aligned top stitching*

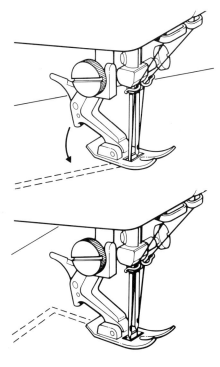

Figure 42 *Turning a corner with a twin needle*

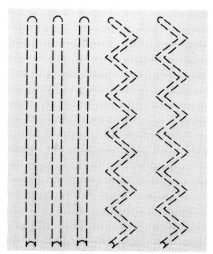

Figure 43 *To evenly space well-separated pin tucks, use a quilting guide. Right, tricot stitch gives a more decorative pin tuck*

Most fully-automatic machines will take a **twin needle** but it seems to be the most neglected of all needles available. If you are worried about using the twin then go back to your consultant and ask him or her to *show* you how to use it: it is surprisingly simple and once you have sewn with it I am sure you will have many uses for the twin rows of stitches produced. It is ideal for a double top-stitching line – which is *always* evenly spaced – and for special embroidery effects. (Note: older machines or new side-loading models will not normally take a twin needle.)

Twin needle sewing (Figure 41) is straightforward. The needle fits into the machine like any other because it has *one* shank to insert into the needle clamp. Thread the machine with the two threads by placing the two 'cotton reels' on to the two thread spindles: holding *both threads together* go through the threading system, separating only to go through the tension discs and the thread guides above the needle – and of course the two eyes! Set the machine on straight stitch and start to sew: there will be two rows of straight lines on top of the fabric and a zig-zag underneath because, of course, there is only *one* bobbin thread underneath to keep the two top ones in place.

Because of the width of the needle it is necessary to restrict the needle swing when doing zig-zag or embroidery stitches. Refer to the handbook with your machine for guidance – usually the maximum width setting would be about '3' because of the width of the needle, though, the pattern will still be '5'. Wider-swing machines will obviously have greater flexibility.

To turn a corner (Figure 42) with the twin needle: stop stitching and using the balance wheel just pierce the fabric with the left-hand needle (this is slightly longer than the right-hand one). Turn the fabric through 45 degrees. Take *one* stitch, leaving the left-hand needle piercing the fabric again and turn the fabric another 45 degrees. Continue sewing.

It is fun to experiment with zig-zag and utility stitches and then move on to embroidery patterns to see what effects can be obtained. Two threads the same colour will give a different effect to two toning shades and a different one again will be produced by two contrasting colours, or try one metallic/lurex thread with a normal thread. Try two threads of different thickness – there are many permutations.

Some of the patterns will look better than others so it is a good idea to add samples to your folder with some written comments on how you achieved the desired effect.

Machine pin tucks are sewn equally easily with the twin needle. The machine is set up in the normal way for twin-needle sewing but the *bobbin tension is increased considerably*: when you stitch the bobbin thread pulls the two top threads closely together, causing a ridge in the fabric. A quick tip here is to do a centre row of stitches, then place the edge of the foot next to the line of stitches already sewn and sew another line. Continue in this way, moving across the piece to be tucked, *always sewing in the same direction!*

Figure 44 *Pin tucks sewn with the twin needle*

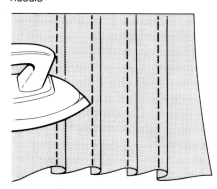

A woven fabric can be pressed with the tucks all facing in the same direction. A knitted fabric looks quite effective when the tucks are left unpressed.

To ensure tucks further apart are evenly spaced use the quilting guide and for a more decorative pin tuck use the tricot stitch (three-step zig-zag).

A triple needle (Figure 45) can be inserted into a limited number of machines. Most of the comments on twin needles apply to triples but before purchase check that your machine will take this type of needle.

The wing needle (Figure 46) is also very much neglected. Use for a hem-stitch finish (the wings enlarge the hole). Other stitches can have particularly good effects with this needle. Experiment with your own range of stitches.

Threads and fabrics

There are a wide variety of threads available now for the home dressmaker and craftworker. Most work well in the sewing machine and some have, in fact, been designed specifically for modern fabrics and machines. Most machines sew perfectly happily with most threads but occasionally a certain make of thread will be rejected by a machine. If your machine has been sewing perfectly well up until this particular project look to your thread before anything else. Put another make/type of thread into your machine and often it will revert to perfect stitching again. Most ladies buy thread by *colour*: they require an excellent match between thread and fabric and so select from the various makes available within the type of thread they want to use, e.g. polyester thread, combination thread or a pure silk or cotton. When you find a thread that you and your machine like using it is a reasonably good idea to look first to that particular brand's colour range. Be on the alert, however, for *new* products to try out and experiment with.

Without reviewing all the threads on the market by trade names, here are some general guidelines.

Pure fabrics/fibres (cotton, silk, wool) can be sewn with 100 per cent cotton '40' or '50'. On silk and wool try 100 per cent silk thread for a pleasant sewing experience and a professional finish (available from larger or specialist shops selling Gütterman). Pure fabrics can also be sewn with all-purpose thread – but watch the thickness of the threads because they do vary from one manufacturer to another.

Nylons, polyesters and other **synthetics** *must* be sewn with a synthetic thread and there are many to choose from. It is most important to have a certain amount of g-i-v-e or s-t-r-e-t-c-h in the thread to match that of the fabric. Also use these polyester threads on jerseys, stretch towelling, plush and knits so that the seams will not pop when you stretch or bend.

Combination fabrics – wool/polyester, polyester/cotton and so on – can be sewn with most threads but if there is more than a small percentage of polyester, favour a polyester or a combination thread. There is a poly/cotton thread available from Coats which is ideal for heavier cotton and linen mixes. Sylko Supreme is a mercerized cotton thread wrapped around a polyester core which is in fact ideal for polyesters, combination and pure fabrics.

As a complete contrast – threads used just to embellish your garments can break all the rules! Compare threads to achieve the effect you are looking for. Anchor do a fine machine embroidery cotton in a variety of plain and random colours. From this, fine polyesters, combination thread, medium cottons, pure silk to buttonhole twist and bold threads you can have an amazing choice. Gold, silver, lurex and combination threads for embroidery are available from specialist shops.

Just remember that the modern precision-made sewing machine will not normally take heavy threads on top *and* in the bobbin – there just is not

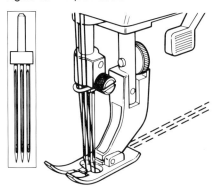

Figure 45 A triple needle

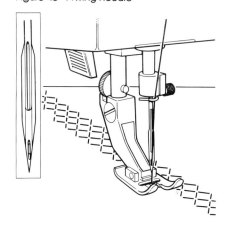

Figure 46 A wing needle

Figure 47 Soft and silky jerseys need special care and special techniques. Courtesy Vogue Patterns

Figure 48 Put slight hand tension on silky jersey when machining

Figure 49 Striped fabric used to excellent effect. Extra special care is needed with cutting out and sewing. Courtesy Butterick

enough room in the raceway – so do leave a finer thread on the bobbin if you are using a buttonhole twist on the top.

For problems with thread cops, mis-threading etc., see the next chapter.

Difficult fabrics

Very sheer fabrics benefit from support whilst sewing. The new Vilene 'sew and tear' tears away from the stitches with the greatest of ease.

To ensure the fabric of the yoke, cuff, pocket, etc. stays smooth *always* support the fabric before you start to sew with a Vilene or other suitable interfacing/backing fabric. In many instances in garment-making the Vilene can be left inside, hidden away. If the small design is on a large piece of fabric not normally interfaced, place a piece of Vilene behind the design, stitch, then tear or cut away the surplus Vilene around the motif when it is completed.

Silky jerseys give the most headaches. Try these tips which *combined* will solve most of the problems:

- Wherever possible use the straight-stitch presser foot rather than the zig-zag foot.
- Use a slightly longer straight-stitch length than usual and *never* the straight stretch-stitch seam (¦¦¦) – keep that for heavier jerseys.
- Use a ballpoint or scarfed needle.
- Use a synthetic or *fine* multi-purpose thread (e.g. Sylko Supreme).
- Use *invisible* zippers whenever possible – they are particularly marvellous on this type of fabric.
- Put slight tension on the fabric (Figure 48) by pulling it *very slightly* just in front of the needle with the right hand – not enough to distort the stitch length – and with the left hand hold the fabric behind the needle so that it is slightly taut.

Heavier jersey fabric and **double knits** can be sewn with the variety of stretch and knit stitches available on automatic machines (see the section on stretch stitches in Chapter 3 for more details). If you only have zig-zag then try using a width of '1' for seams – this will give a very slight ease in the seam. Use a synthetic or multi-purpose thread.

Jumper knits and **hand-knits** can be sewn with the stretch seam and overcast available on many modern machines. Feather stitch is also excellent for seaming because it is very stretchy and the formation of the stitches will allow unwanted fabric to be trimmed away without the knitting unravelling. Some machines incorporate a specific 'knit stitch' which is excellent and on some overlockers seaming, overlocking and trimming is possible with excellent results.

When matching **plaids** and **stripes** – providing they are cut out correctly! – hold pieces together with pins across ↔ the seam line, sew over the pins for accurate matching. This will not damage the machine.

Velvets and plush will not 'creep' on their pile during sewing if you use a roller foot. A Teflon foot or 'even-feed' foot will give similar results.

Leather and **PVC** also benefit from the roller foot and the Teflon foot was designed to glide over these surfaces.

There are some really wonderful new fabrics on the market. Even some experts have problems differentiating between fabulous silky polyesters and the real 100 per cent article. Modern methods can give new synthetic mixtures the bulk and feel of wools and tweeds. Not only this, but adding polyester to natural fibres will give greater durability and crease resistance without altering the feel of the cloth.

I must include a sad fact: with all these innovations it is little wonder that elderly sewing machines often cannot cope – they were made in a different era for a different basic ingredient. So: if you have an old machine, stick to fabrics you know it can cope with – if you want to broaden your scope and use the latest fabrics, invest in the latest machines and haute couture will be at your fingertips.

Figure 50 *Leather of all kinds poses no problem to the modern machine. Courtesy Vogue Patterns and Butterick*

Table 3 Needles, threads and fabrics

Fabrics	Type		Threads	Machine needle continental	Machine needle British
Fine fabrics such as net, organdie, lace, lawn, voile, chiffon, tulle, silk	Natural		Sylko No. 50 or Sylko Supreme	60–70	9–11
	Man-made		Gütterman or Sylko Supreme	60–70	9–11
Lightweight fabrics such as gingham, muslin, fine poplin, taffeta, silk, seersucker crêpe de chine, wool challis, faille	Natural		Sylko No. 50 or Sylko Supreme	70–90 scarfed	11–14
	Man-made and mixtures		Sylko Supreme or Gütterman	70–90 scarfed	11–14
Mediumweight fabrics such as poplin, cotton, suitings, corduroy, linen, satin, brocade, velvet, raw silks, wool crêpe, bouclé	Natural		Sylko No. 40 or Sylko Supreme	70–90 scarfed	11–14
	Man-made and mixtures		Gütterman or Sylko Supreme	70–90 scarfed	11–14
Heavyweight fabrics such as tweed, gaberdine, flannel, sailcloth, twill, denim, canvas, furnishings	Natural		Sylko No. 40 or Sylko Supreme	90–110	14–18
	Man-made and mixtures		Sylko Supreme	90–110	14–18
Stretch fabrics Use stretch stitch wherever possible Silk and cotton jersey, polyester jersey, single and double knits, plush, stretch towelling	Lightweight	Natural	Sylko No. 50 + stretch stitch otherwise Sylko Supreme	60–70 ball or scarfed	9–11 ball or scarfed
		Man-made and mixtures	Sylko Supreme or Gütterman	60–70 ball or scarfed	9–11 ball or scarfed
	Heavyweight	Natural	Sylko No. 40 + stretch stitch otherwise Sylko Supreme	70–90 ball or scarfed	11–14 ball or scarfed
		Man-made and mixtures	Sylko Supreme or Gütterman	70–90 ball or scarfed	11–14 ball or scarfed
Special fabrics	PVC	Man-made	Sylko Supreme	90–100	14–16
	Suede/leather and imitation	Natural	Sylko No. 40 or strong thread	Spear or 90–110	14–18
		Man-made	Sylko Supreme	leather point	
Also: Pure silks and pure medium and heavyweight wools	Natural		Gütterman pure silk thread	70–90	11–14
Top stitching Lightweight fabrics	All types		Sylko No. 40 or 50 or Sylko Supreme	60–90 scarfed or ball if appropriate	9–14 scarfed or ball if appropriate
Medium fabrics	All types		Sylko No. 40 or 50 or Sylko Supreme 2 threads	90–110	14–18
Heavy fabrics	All types		Bold or Gütterman button twist	90–110	14–18

Chapter 7
Problems

Few sewers are lucky enough to have a sewing room or area where they can leave out their machines and often the sewing machine is brought out hurriedly for a short sewing session.

Haste is the mother and father of many problems! Formulate your own check-list of needles, threads, tensions, stitch selection and so on.

Always thread the machine slowly and carefully – even when you are used to it, because in haste it is so easy to mis-thread!

So however hard-pressed you are for time it will help to thread the machine with care, go quickly through your check-list and thus you can save spending all your precious sewing time finding out why the machine will not work.

It is truly amazing how many ladies *refuse to consider* that *they* might have inserted the needle wrongly, or mis-threaded through the 'system'! Usually it is the simple and obvious things that cause the problems. Even if you have been sewing away for many, many years you must make allowances for differences between your new and old model. It is a fact that most complaints with new machines are proved to be such a simple error by the user so you can appreciate why the stores and the manufacturers quiz you when they receive complaints – they are not unhelpful or necessarily suspicious of your motives, they are professional people with a desire to help the customer and protect their good name. So, if you have a genuine complaint please do approach the company concerned, but not until you have thoroughly investigated and tested the machine yourself.

Some problems arise because thread cops or reels spin – particularly when sewing quite fast (e.g. long straight seams) and/or when doing a lot of stopping and starting. Ensure that you have the little red felt cushion on the spindle for your cotton reel to bounce on: it makes for much smoother unravelling. The take-up lever can cause a spin by a jerky start – particularly if it is down when you try to start the machine by depressing the foot pedal. Try to cultivate the habit of glancing at the lever and if necessary turn the balance wheel by hand to raise the lever to its highest position before putting your foot down. (Incidentally – *always, always* turn the balance wheel *towards* you – never away from you.)

The opposite of a spin – a complete stop or jerk – also causes problems: in fact the repercussion can be serious because a violent jerk can jam the machine totally and this is a problem that will result in an engineer's call and that can be expensive. This problem usually occurs during fast sewing (again long, straight seams) and with a cotton reel/cop which has a nick cut into the edge to secure the loose end of thread. During sewing the thread is dashing up and down the reel, the reel is probably 'dancing' a little on the spindle and suddenly the thread and the nick catch together and it does in fact stop the thread moving for a second – quite long enough to do damage. When using this kind of cotton reel make sure that the nick is at the *base* of the spindle and the problem is most unlikely to occur. The long thin cops do not have a nick but sometimes the top is a little rough and the same problem occurs – have an emery board amongst your sewing kit and do a little smoothing if necessary.

When you have a machine where you insert the bobbin into a bobbin case and then put both into the raceway you *must* put the bobbin into the case correctly. In a survey on this one little point it was amazing how many ladies could not remember how they inserted their bobbins into the case (clockwise or anti-clockwise) and also had no idea that it made any difference to their sewing. It can happen that you will get a spool spin if the bobbin is wrongly inserted so it is worth checking on this.

It can be infuriating if your thread starts to split and unravel between the needle and the take-up lever. Normally it is not a bad reel of thread but a roughness somewhere on the needle or the machine that the thread is rubbing against. First, change your needle because the eye can be rough. If this does not cure the problem then check all the thread guides very carefully and see if one has a burr – resort to the emery treatment again if you find the roughness. Alternatively, perhaps one of the little wire guides has got slightly squashed and is not allowing the thread through easily. With your tiniest screwdriver *very* carefully enlarge the area that the thread passes through.

If your machine seems totally dead: check the fuse in the plug before reaching for the phone to call in the repair man: it can save time and money!

Chapter 8
Overlockers

The professional finish by the industrial overlock machines has long been coveted by the machinist at home. Recent technological advances have perfected an amazing variety of overcasting/overlock-type stitches for domestic machines: these are quick and simple to perform and are ideal and perfectly adequate for finishing off both dressmaking and craftwork.

Even with these facilities semi-professional and expert dressmakers still agitated for the professional overlocker to neaten *and* cut or trim the fabric in one operation. By constantly badgering the trade they managed to get manufacturers interested in their needs. Once on the market interest became even more acute and now most manufacturers can offer at least one overlocker and some offer two-, three- and four-thread models.

Figure 51 *Velour sweatshirting and other sportswear fabrics are sewn to perfection with the overlocker. Courtesy Butterick*

Figure 52 *Example of a four-thread domestic overlocker*

1. Foldaway carrying handle
2. Thread guides
3. Tension control for chain stitch
4. Thread guides
5. Thread take-up
6. Thread guide
7. Bed
8. Side cover
9. Needle plate
10. Stitch control lever
11. Threading chart
12. Thread guide pole
13. Tension control for overlock stitch
14. Thread guides
15. Spool pin
16. Spool holder
17. Extension plate
18. Thread stand
19. Tension control for overlock stitch looper
20. Tension control for chain stitch looper
21. Hand wheel
22. Plug connector socket
23. Light and power switch
24. Front cover release lever
25. Front cover
26. Foot control
27. Accessory case

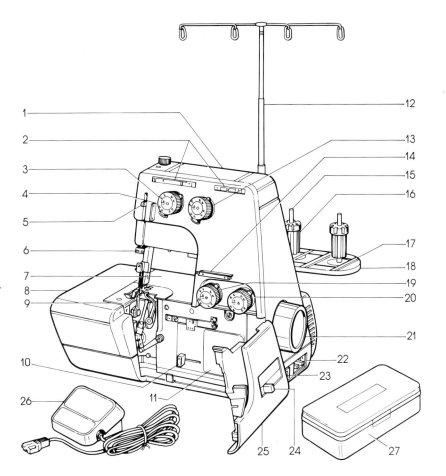

28. Rear needle for overlock stitch
29. Front needle for chain stitch
30. Presser foot
31. Fixed cutter
32. Presser foot lever
33. Thread cutter
34. Double chain stitch looper
35. Overlock stitch looper
36. Moving cutter
37. Thread take-up

Front and side covers opened

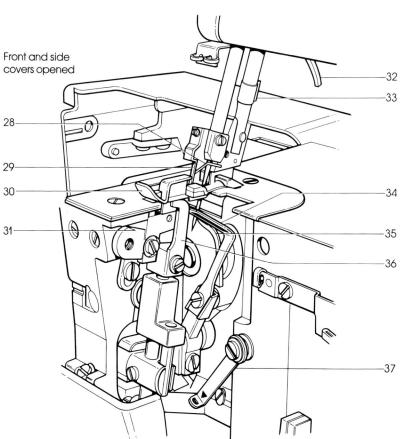

Domestic overlockers are neat, streamlined and compact machines 300 to 350 mm (12 to 14 inches) square which would grace any sewing room. As with normal machines a few have a light over the needle (look for this feature). Two makes actually use standard domestic needles — not specialist ones — which is helpful. Some models are easier to thread than others but all will take a large variety of threads and will hold 500- or 1000-metre (or more!) cops which is important with these machines because they eat up thread at an amazing rate. Test the weight if that is important to you because weight does vary enormously, and look out for models with a carry-handle. Check for extras and attachments because the latest breed of overlockers will do a lot more than just neaten edges and various needle plates and presser feet are supplied for specialist tasks. See Figure 52.

Overlockers come in two-, three- and four-thread varieties and can use one or two needles. Often the number of threads used is in the manufacturer's logo — i.e. Frister Lock 3 (a three-thread model). The number of threads used gives different stitches and techniques and these will be illustrated below. A two-thread machine will have limited uses compared to a four-thread, but a four-thread can use two, three or four threads as required.

All the threads are 'top' threads — you do not have a bobbin on an overlocker. One thread is a 'needle' thread and another goes through a hook-like prong under the needle plate (called a 'looper'): these together produce a chain and/or over-edge looped stitches. Additional threads can provide for a second needle, give a seam plus looped overlock, a double seam and looped overlock, intricate overlocking with multi-threads, etc.

Four-thread overlocks

There are two types of four-thread overlocks. The most usual is one producing a two-thread double chain stitch and a two-thread overlock. These can be used separately or together to produce a combination safety stitch.

Another form of four-thread overlock (such as the Frister Knit-Lock 5), uses all four threads to overlock, two of which are parallel rows of straight stitch, which are invaluable in holding the edges of even the most loosely knitted material firmly and securely in place.

Fortunately, despite all the various thread and needle permutations the overlockers are easy to thread up and all makes have graphic charts to follow both in the handbooks and on the machines themselves. Many are colour- or symbol-coded as are the tension dials: each thread has its own tension unit. See Figures 57 and 58.

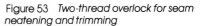

Figure 53 *Two-thread overlock for seam neatening and trimming*

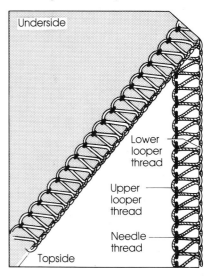

Figure 54 *Three-thread overlock provides a seam and neatens and trims edges*

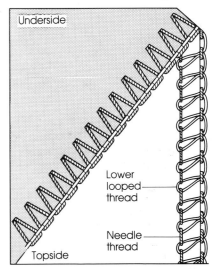

Figure 55 *Four-thread combination stitch*

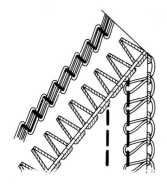

Figure 56 *A form of four-thread overlock stitch which secures the edges of the most loosely-knitted material*

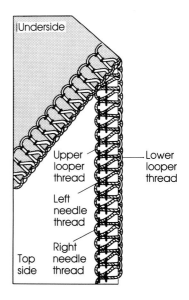

Figure 57 *Example of a threading chart printed on the machine*

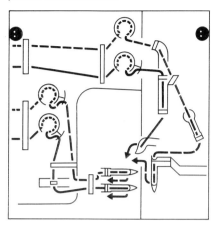

Figure 58 *Example of an overlock threading system, showing looper threads*

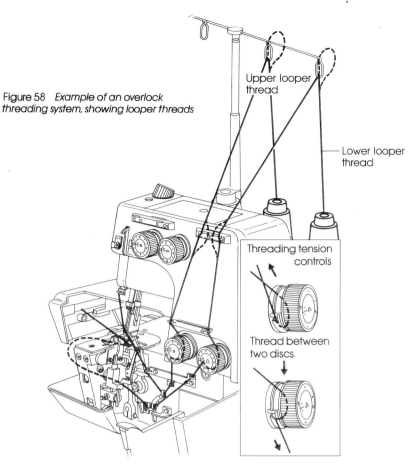

Figure 59 *The presser foot is not raised at the end of stitching. Just feed in the next piece of fabric as needed*

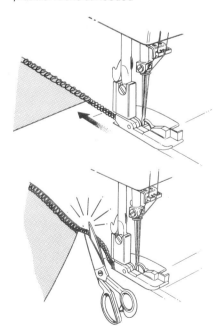

Once threaded a few centimetres of 'chain' are run off: test the machine with a spare piece of fabric and check tensions. On reaching the end of the fabric continue to sew for a few centimetres and then snip with scissors.

It should be noted that most overlockers sew very much faster than normal domestic machines – approximately 1500 stitches per minute.

Stitch widths and lengths can be varied in different ways depending on models. Some require small screwdriver adjustment, some use a different needle-plate. Some widths are merely controlled by using the left or right needle. All systems are straightforward. Refer to your manufacturer's handbook for exact details.

Overlockers do not merely neaten. A wide variety of other techniques is being perfected for these useful little machines.

Figure 60 *Example of tension adjustment and their uses*

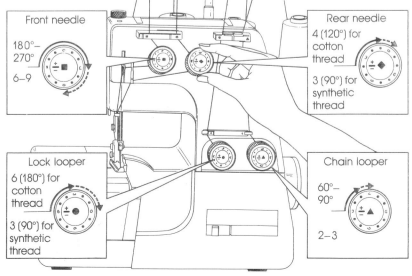

Some provide amazing s-t-r-e-t-c-h on knits, jersey fabrics and hand knitteds and are a boon to the domestic knitting machine users, enabling the garment to be assembled as quickly and easily as it was to knit.

Wool, acrylic and other such yarns can be used on the overlockers with ease – so too can the variety of lurex and metallic yarns and threads available.

Cops of 500 m and 1000 m in Sylko are ideal for dressmaking needs, and indeed some manufacturers provide even longer metrage.

Special effects and finishes on heavier fabrics, denims, leather, PVC and so on can be obtained with bold and buttonhole twist and pure silk threads. Because each thread has its own tension control various threads can be used together – superb for craftworkers.

By adjusting stitch width/length and tension (Figure 60) a really excellent rolled edge is possible for flimsy or lingerie fabrics and scarves. If you are using a soft jersey fabric *pull* it firmly during sewing and you will get the expensive looking *lettuce edging* widely used in ready-to-wear. Wonderful for the silky jerseys for day, evening or nightwear. See Figure 61(a).

Using a slightly different stitch sequence and width a tiny shell edge is also effortless. Use for lingerie, babywear and also as a nice touch for edging linings. See Figure 61(b).

Narrow or wide, it is effective to produce rows and rows of tucks in matching or contrasting threads – all will be neat and evenly produced (Figure 62).

With the two-thread overlock stitch an intriguing and attractive abutted seam is obtained. Align the two fabrics with their undersides facing each other. Overlock along the edge and *unfold* and flatten the seam – press (Figure 63).

Figure 61
(a) Rolled hem
(b) Shell hem

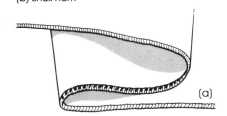

Figure 62 *Overlocker tucks*

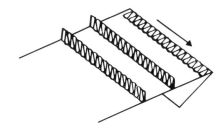

Figure 63 *Overlocker abutted seams*

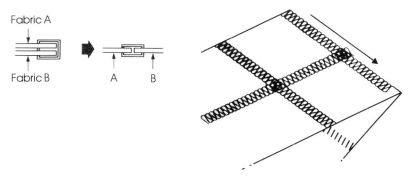

Some machines will sew decorative and utility double chain stitch, (Figure 64) which is useful for dress and/or crafts *without*, cutting the fabric This is achieved by adding a special plate attachment and/or removing or dropping the cutters.

Decorative braid (Figure 65) can be attractive and is done by sewing over a plain cord, braid or ribbon.

Figure 64 *Overlocker chain stitch*

Figure 65 *Overlocker braid stitch*

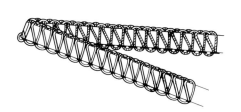

Figure 66   Overlockers can stitch a cord into jersey or knit materials to prevent seams stretching

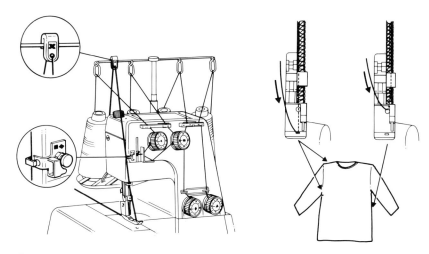

A corded overlock can be attractive but is also used to strengthen or to *prevent* stretch in shoulder, side or sleeve seams. A filler cord is sewn into the garment with the overlocking. See Figure 66.

Although many domestic sewing machines now incorporate a blind hem it is in fact not an invisible hem as many people would like. However, an invisible blind hem is possible on the overlocker: not only that, but, of course, the fabric is trimmed at the same time. Figure 67 shows clearly the special presser foot and the sewing operation. The screw on the foot is used to alter the stitch width. This really does work and is excitingly effective!

Figure 67   An invisible blind hem made on an overlocker
(a) The folding
(b) The combined stitching and trimming
(c) The finished hem

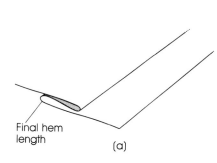

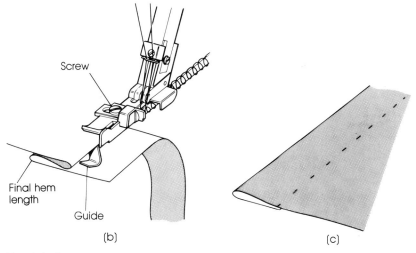

New into the country (Figure 68) is another presser foot for attaching elastic (i.e. knicker elastic) on to fabrics. This amazing technique enables the elastic to be sewn on, fabric edges overlocked and trimmed, with tension applied so that the fabric is gathered on to the elastic (or the elastic stretched on to the fabric) at the same time. A totally new concept for the home sewer producing an elasticized finish only comparable to mass-produced lingerie items. The tension control screw on the front of the foot is easily adjusted to vary the elasticity.

Figure 68   A presser foot used to apply elastic

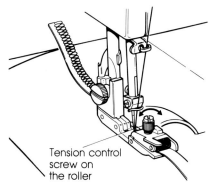

Care for your machine

Like all machines a little love and care will give good results and help to extend its life.

Because of the rapid stitching fluff will accumulate in quite large quantities so keep dusting out around the cutting blades and needle areas with a nice tufty brush.

Make sure you insert the needle(s) the correct way around: refer to your manufacturer's handbook.

Keep the machine well oiled to ensure smooth sewing: refer to the manufacturer's handbook for diagrams of oiling points. But do not over-oil, as this could stain your materials. After oiling always run the machine (without thread or fabric) to ensure oil is evenly distributed throughout the bearings.

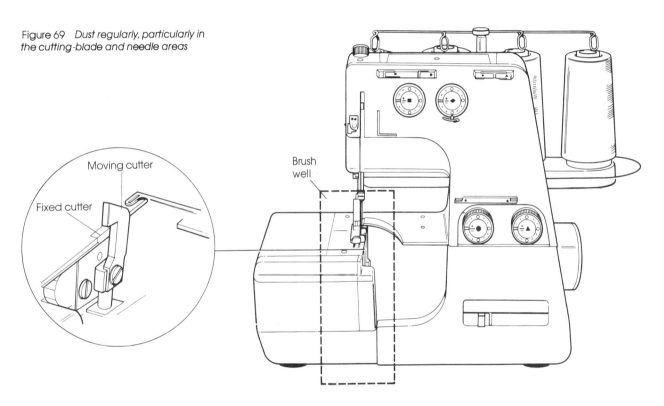

Figure 69 *Dust regularly, particularly in the cutting-blade and needle areas*

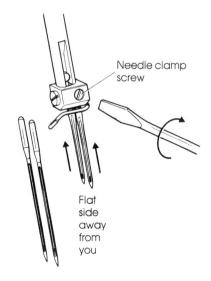

Figure 70 *Fitting needles*

The Combi

A quite revolutionary machine is worth noting in this chapter. The Combi is both a domestic sewing machine (incorporating a good selection of automatic stitches and the automatic buttonhole, etc.) and a two-thread overlocker in *one machine*.

From the front it appears quite normal (needle at the left and balance wheel at the right) but when overlocking is required the machine is turned around and the overlocker is on the 'other end'.

All the features of the machine are described in other chapters because general comments on automatic machines apply to this machine. The uses of two-thread overlock have also been described.

For the dedicated dressmaker or someone with limited space the Combi (from New Home) is worth investigation.

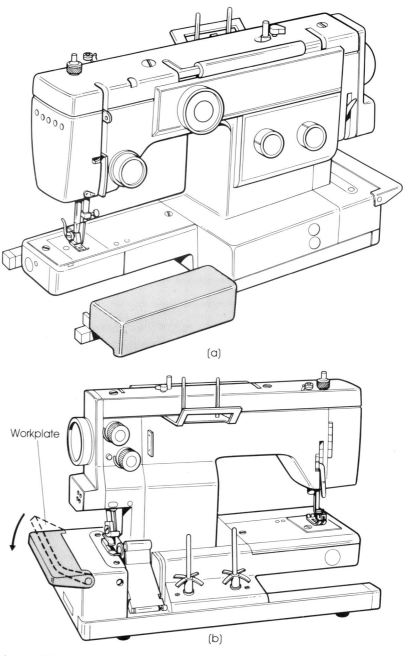

Figure 71 *From the front (a) the Combi looks like a normal domestic machine but from the back (b) you see it includes a two-thread overlocker*
New Home sewing machines

My special thanks to Frister Rossman for help, guidance and illustrations for this chapter.

Chapter 9
Computer sewing

With the tremendous scope and capabilities of mechanical machines and with so many excellent ones on the market what can be so very special about the up-market computer machines? What, too, are the *differences* when one starts dabbling in this new and exciting area of technology?

Everything I have discussed so far will apply to the computer machine, i.e. stitches, techniques and various uses – and how to come to grips with, and learn about, your machine. Now we will go into the realm of microchips and describe various things that are unique to these technologically wonderful and advanced machines.

Certain features are apparent in all the computers but, as with all products, each manufacturer strives for individuality and supremacy. I will describe points pertaining to all machines, very special features of machines I have tested and give a comparison chart for easy reference (Table 4).

At the time of compiling this book there are six companies retailing computer machines: Frister Rossman, Jones & Brother, New Home, Pfaff, Singer, and Viking/Husqvarna. Some have produced more than one computer machine, so great have been advances in technology in the early eighties. Development has been a major research feature of all companies and this new breed of machine has been tried and tested to unlimited and undreamed of heights. The microchip actually means less moving parts to go wrong, thus increasing efficiency. It also means that any fault that *might* possibly occur can be easily traced: some machines have a built-in computer to fault-find and 'tell' the mechanic. However, as with other major innovations (e.g. microwave cooking), do be prepared to look at these machines through new eyes and remember when you are sewing – the sky's the limit!

Figure 72   *All around the house ... you can use your computer machine for so many things. Courtesy New Home*

Figure 73 The Memory Craft machine will sew the twenty-six letters of the alphabet and numbers 0 to 9 in script or in block print. Words and entire sentences can be programmed, including punctuation marks

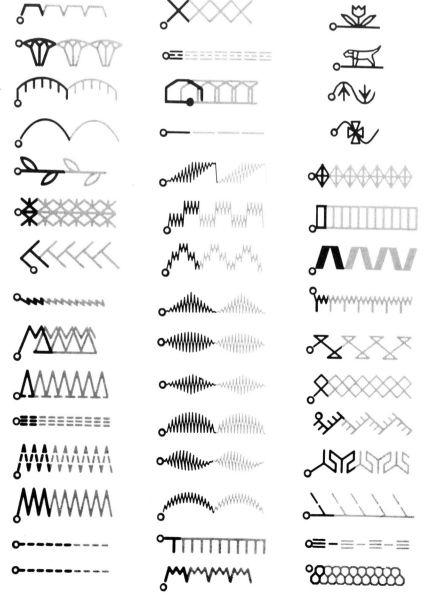

Figure 74 Example of some stitches/patterns in the Memory Craft. The bold lines on the chart indicate the unit of each pattern sewn when the memory button is touched once, thus in pattern combinations this is the stitch sequence 'joined on' to the next pattern programmed. The pattern can be varied by manually changing the stitch length and stitch width. Each pattern starts at 'o'

So the main feature is microchip technology controlling the machine rather than control by levers, knobs and dials. This means that *exact* and *perfect results* are obtained *every time* you program your machine. Each stitch or pattern on the machine is programmed so that on selection of the pattern the stitch length and width are determined too – three steps in one. At the present time there are three methods of selecting stitches/patterns:

1   Push buttons and LED indication beside an image on a display panel
2   Numerical digital selection (by push button)
3   Sensorized touch control panel

All methods are successful and a decision here is one of personal choice.

Stitch patterns are usually grouped into helpful sections – e.g. stretch sewing, construction stitches, craft stitches, embroidery stitches – and are sometimes colour-coded as well.

All machines have over-ride for stitch width and length control should the operator wish to make manual adjustments.

When a pattern is programmed the machine will always start sewing at the *beginning* of the design. See Figure 74.

Mirror image is also a general feature: this enables the pattern to be 'turned over' or reversed. See Figure 75.

Figure 75   *Computer samples. Mirror (reversed) image is a useful feature on computer machines*

Buttonholes can be remembered and thus reproduced exactly the same time after time, although some makes do utilize a special presser foot into which you insert the button to gauge the length instead of putting it into memory.

Needle penetration is exactly controlled so that when the foot pedal is depressed the thrust of the needle will be the same whether a very flimsy fabric or ten layers of denim are being sewn. This obviously makes sewing easier and gives a more professional finish.

All the machines tested had quick and easy one-hand threading and clip-on/off feet; converted to free-arm use; took a twin needle; and had a good selection of basic stitches for dressmaking and some for embroidery. Most machines self-selected normal straight stitch when turned on (one machine selected zig-zag) and all but one cancel out your own sequence when turned off.

Most machines will stop sewing in the needle-up position – a really good sewing aid. One-stitch-at-a-time control was achieved without problem with all models by depressing the foot control. The foot pedals varied in size and depth quite dramatically but none posed problems.

Some machines had drop-in bobbins (some inserted first into a bobbin case), all worked successfully and were jam-proof. The drop-in bobbins and the machines with the alarm light were the easiest for judging when more bobbin thread was required.

All the machines produced all stitches without constant alterations to tensions; however, the Lynx and the Prima have self-adjusting tension with their basic Guide cassette (Figure 76).

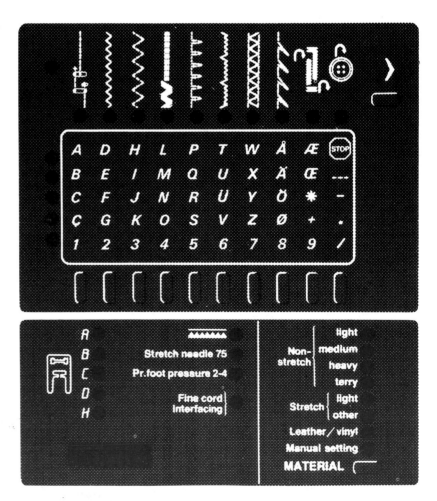

Figure 76 *Control cassette inserted in the Frister Rossman Lynx to produce alphabet and numbers*

Computer sewing

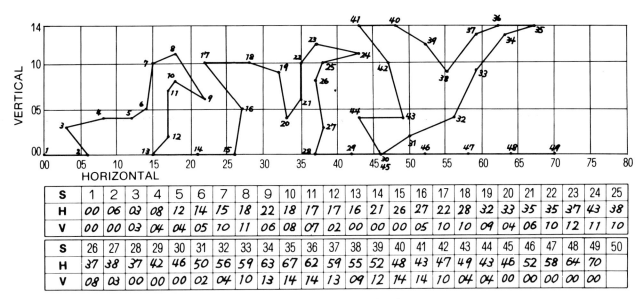

S	1	2	3	4	5	6	7	8	9	10	11	12	13	14	15	16	17	18	19	20	21	22	23	24	25
H	00	06	03	08	12	14	15	18	22	18	17	17	16	21	26	27	22	28	32	33	35	35	37	43	38
V	00	00	03	04	04	05	10	11	06	08	07	02	00	00	00	05	10	10	09	04	06	10	12	11	10

S	26	27	28	29	30	31	32	33	34	35	36	37	38	39	40	41	42	43	44	45	46	47	48	49	50
H	37	38	37	42	46	50	56	59	63	67	62	59	55	52	48	43	47	49	43	46	52	58	64	70	
V	08	03	00	00	00	02	04	10	13	14	14	13	09	12	14	14	10	04	04	00	00	00	00	00	

All machines tested (except the Singer 2010) could be programmed by the user to produce his or her own sequence of stitches. This is termed as putting patterns into memory and this phrase will often be repeated as you read on. Each time a pattern, letter or number is put into memory it counts as 'one memory'. Thus a machine writing 'VOGUE' would use five letters and thus five memories! Table 4 shows the number of memories achieved by a particular machine.

Figure 77 *A program sheet for the Jones & Brother Galaxie*

Figure 78 *The first talking computer sewing machine, the Jones & Brother Galaxie*

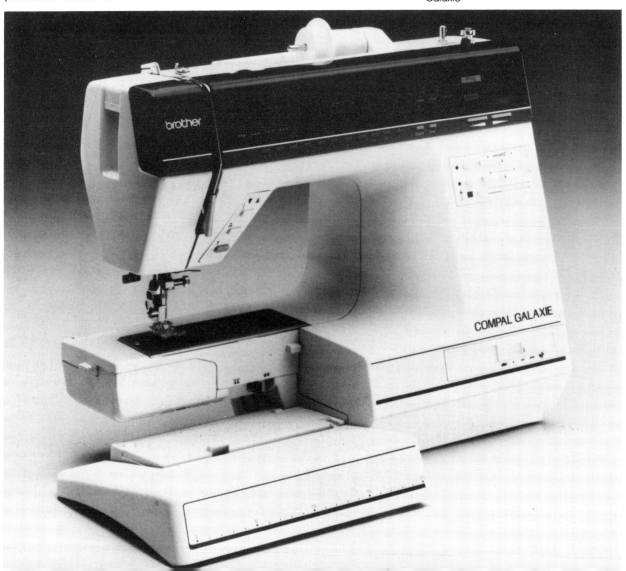

All machines had a full selection of presser feet to do specialist techniques such as overlocking, buttonholes, hemming, zippers and cording.

All machines were tested using Sylko Supreme and Gütterman threads, and bold or buttonhole twist.

Remembering that all the machines tested incorporate the foregoing data, here are some extra-special features about each of them:

With the Frister Rossman Lynx good attention was given to details of particular importance for dressmaking. The computer was programmed to anticipate many sewing requirements so on insertion of the Guide cassette and the pressing of the appropriate button to indicate fabric in use, the machine self-selected a suitable stitch, appropriate width and length, adjusted the tension as necessary and told which presser foot was needed. A selection of embroidery patterns, alphabets and numbers are included on other cassettes – easily inserted and easy to program with up to twenty-five memories for patterns and fifty-two for letters (Figure 76).

The first *talking* machine, the Galaxie produced by Jones & Brother (Figure 78), announced in an extremely clear voice if the user had set the controls incorrectly, an amazing sewing aid for the beginner and new users of this machine. Completely operable without the foot pedal by just using hand controls, it would prove a boon to handicapped users in particular. The sliding variable-speed control was excellent and another special feature, the side-cutter, trimmed the fabric whilst overlocking on woven and knitted fabrics. Although a large selection of stitches is available they cannot be 'mixed' by the user. However, a feature of the Galaxie is that the operator's own designs can be fed into the machine with up to fifty memories in the stitch co-ordinates (see Figure 77). Memorized data can be stored for twenty-four hours *when the machine is switched off* – the only computer machine available for testing with this facility.

Figure 79 *The New Home machine Memory Craft won a blue ribbon at the Daily Mail Ideal Home Exhibition*

Computer sewing

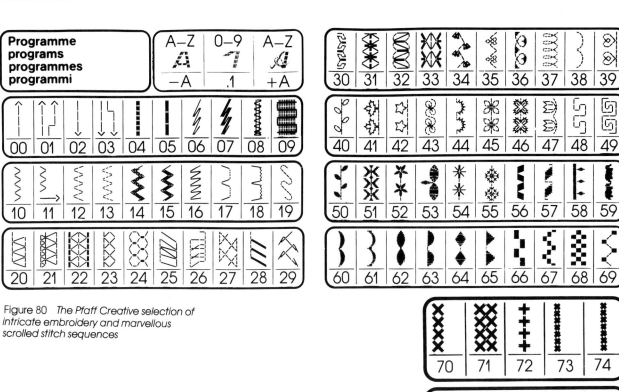

Figure 80 *The Pfaff Creative selection of intricate embroidery and marvellous scrolled stitch sequences*

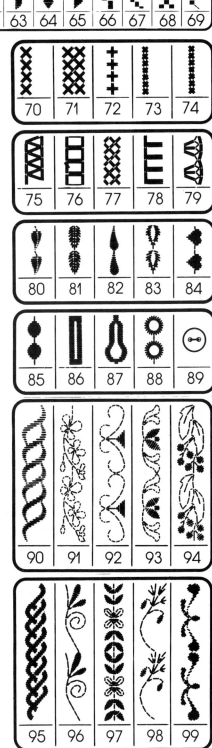

Awarded the *Daily Mail* Blue Ribbon Award at the 1984 *Daily Mail* Ideal Home Exhibition, the New Home Memory Craft provided very high-quality performance and results. A mixture of LED button and digital selection provided working, embroidery and craft stitches, two sets of alphabets, numbers and punctuation marks in script and block capitals. Some patterns could be elongated up to five times their original length – some reduced. Three buttonholes could be memorized: regular, rounded and keyhole. Thirty-one pattern and alphabet memories, complete with editing facility were available. Specialist stitches included a commercial-type overlock, double-edged overcast, basting, saddle stitch, automatic quick-darn, cross stitch and shading stitches for embroidery. Other special features included a beside-the-needle thread cutter, automatic lock-off, unlimited needle positions, needle up/down button, invisible-zipper sewing, large-capacity bobbin and slim foot control.

Also giving high performance, the Pfaff Creative was a compact and lightweight machine incorporating a vast amount of stitchery. Programming was by push-button/digital readout and the sequence ran over a display panel as work progressed. There were sixteen memories for patterns and forty-eight for the two alphabets, correcting facility and memory recall. The large number of programmed stitch patterns included utility, embroidery and craft stitches, alphabets and numbers in block capitals and script, regular and keyhole buttonholes and an eyelet. Specialist stitchery included extremely intricate scrollwork, embroidery patterns, cross stitch, automatic quick-darn, basting, saddle stitching, double tricot stitch and double-edged overcasting. The keyhole buttonhole had seven lengths stored in the computer between 20 and 32 mm, you merely had to program the one required. Other features included monitor warning light for the bobbin, automatic lock-off, needle up or down automatic stop, thirteen needle positions and invisible-zipper sewing.

Since testing the Creative, Pfaff has introduced a machine similar to the Creative in every respect but like the Galaxy it features the facility for the operator to feed in his or her own designs.

Singer produced the Futura 2010 for basic dressmaking techniques and it combined six embroidery stitches and chain stitch which were selected with a 'touch and sew' memory panel on the fascia, but it was not possible for the user to program this machine into various sequences. The bobbin was self-winding through the needle and when it was running low on thread a low-bobbin indicator operated. For buttonholing the button was inserted into the specialist presser foot and the machine self-adjusted to give the perfect size.

58 The Sewing Machine Book

A striking machine in black and silver, the Viking/Husqvarna Prima was made from a carbon fibre material — a spin-off from the space programme. It was particularly quiet, with excellent foot control and perfect embroidery, even on very heavy leather. This machine also took interchangeable cassettes for a full selection of working and embroidery stitches and one other contained block capitals. This was the very first machine to incorporate a *thinking computer* to select stitches and to adjust tensions, stitch widths and lengths according to the fabric being used. It was simple to program (twenty-five pattern memories and fifty for the alphabet), with LED indication and digital over-ride on width and length of stitches, plus thirteen needle positions, automatic lock-off, memory recall, memory corrector button, quick and easy buttonhole which is held in memory, automatic basting, and bobbin thread which can be wound through the needle.

Figure 81 *The Viking/Husqvarna Prima*

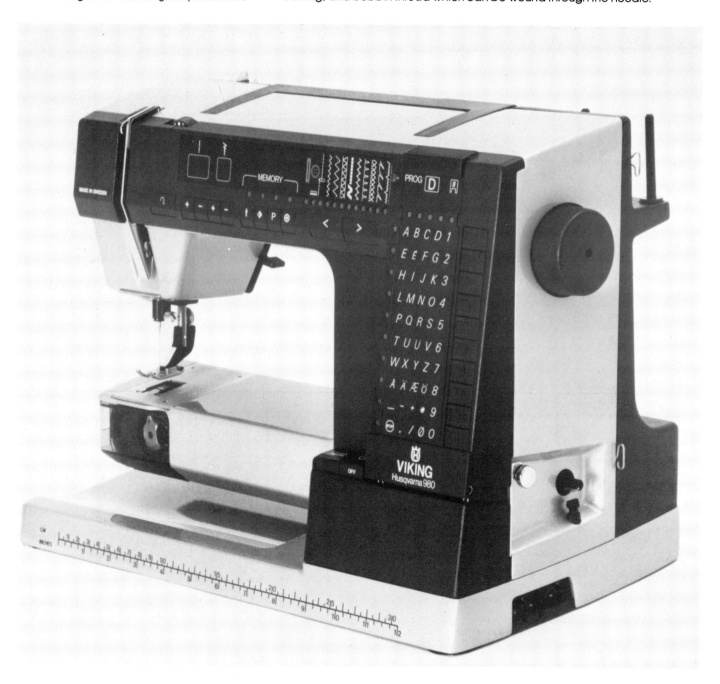

Table 4
Features

Features	Frister Rossman Lynx 880	Jones & Brother Compal Galaxie	New Home Memory Craft	Pfaff Creative 1469	Singer* Futura 2010	Viking/* Husqvarna Prima 980
Needle swing	6 mm	7 mm	7 mm	6 mm	7 mm	6 mm
Type of programming	LED & buttons	LED & buttons	LED & buttons	digital buttons	LED touch panel	LED & buttons
Number of patterns	48 + alphabet	67 + alphabet	51 + alphabet	95 + alphabet	27	51 + alphabet
Number of memories	25 patterns 52 letters	40 on alphabet only	31	16 patterns 48 alphabet	—	25 patterns 52 letters
Alphabet	●	●	×2 script & caps	×2 script & caps		●
Numbers	●	●	●	●		●
Edit facility	corrector		●	corrector		corrector
Buttonholes	1	3 types	3 types	2 types	1	1
Mirror image	●	●	●	●	●	●
Pattern elongation		●	●	●	●	
Pattern reducing			●	●		
Single motif and automatic lock-off	●		●	●	● but no lock-off	●
Memory over-ride	● digital	● some patterns	● dial	● digital	● dials	● digital
Needle-up stop	●	●	●	●		●
Needle-down button	● with pedal	●	●	●		● with pedal
Needle positions (straight stitching)	13	1	unlimited	13	3	13
Automatic lock-off	●		●	●		●
Number of stretch stitches	5	5	10	7	7	7
Double-edge overlock			●	●		
Automatic quick darn			●	●		
Eyelets				●		
Saddle stitching			●	●	●	
Cross stitch			●	●		
Scrollwork embroidery			×1 pattern	×9 patterns		
Basting			●	●	●	●
Back-tack			●			
Cassettes and auto tension	●					●
LED bobbin alarm				●	●	
Bobbin case	● 33 m	●		●		● 30 m
Drop-in bobbin			● 72 m		● 41 m	
Needle threader		●	●		●	
Slow-speed switch		●	●	●	●	
Accessories in machine		●	●	●		
Weight	11.6 kg	11 kg	15 kg	9 kg	14.3 kg	12 kg

LED = Light emitting diode
*Instruction books from manufacturer on request: chargeable

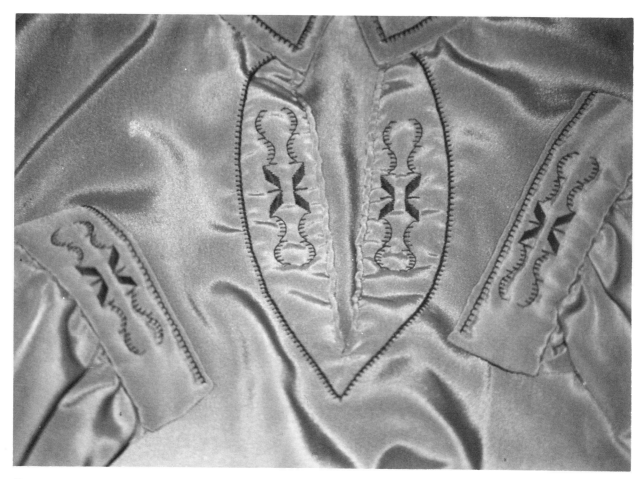

Figure 82 Bold stitching personalizes your garments. Computer sewing by Myra

Figure 83 Fur fabric – a firm favourite with toy-makers and craftworkers. Computer machines will cope with the thickest materials

Computer sewing 61

Figure 84 Superb and elegant Paris original – the quilted jacket has shoulder bands, side panels (no side seams), pockets and pleated sleeve cap. A classic example of updating a traditional craft with the latest fashion design and computer sewing. *Courtesy Vogue Patterns*

Figure 85 Cross stitch is the oldest known embroidery stitch, now perfected on the computer machine. *Courtesy New Home*

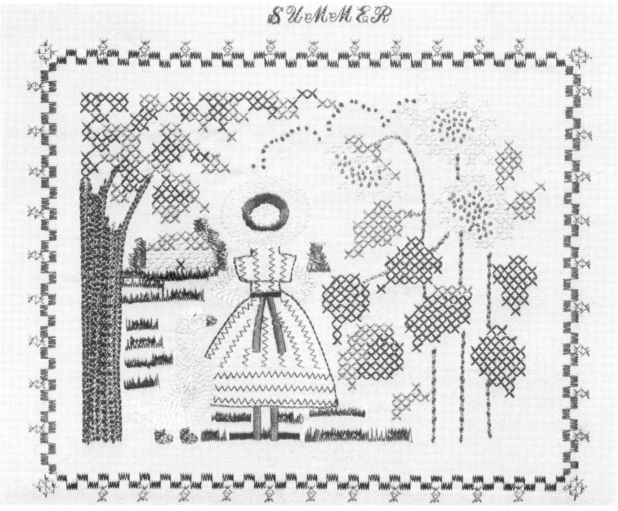

Chapter 10
From witchcraft to wizardry!

At the dawning of civilization skins and cloth were fastened together with crude tools made from fishbones and ivory. In due course man discovered how to make a sewing instrument from iron or bronze and in the fourteenth century someone managed to put an eye in this implement: a needle as we know it had been born. This really was an invention of paramount importance for it is still the basic sewing tool 600 years later. In the centuries that followed, the populace condemned far-sighted inventors trying to perfect a mechanical needle – a sewing 'machine' – to conceive such outrageous ideas was witchcraft, they accused.

It was in a totally different era – the reign of George II – the dawning of the industrial revolution, that Karl Weisenthal, a German, perfected the first machine as we would recognize it. The year was 1750. In England a joiner called Thomas Saint invented a wooden machine in 1790, hoping to manufacture boots and shoes. The construction was crude as was that devised by Barthelemy Thimonier in 1830. Although cumbersome these crude wooden machines were used commercially to produce soldiers' uniforms. At one stage Thimonier's machines were destroyed by angry tailors who imagined that they would be put out of work by the new invention. However, eventually he went back into production with improved machines sewing up to 200 stitches a minute. Both Saint's machine and Thimonier's produced a chain stitch.

In the next century inventive mechanics in America developed the lock-stitch techniques. Although Walter Hunt devised the first lock-stitch design around 1833 it was in 1850 that Blodgett and Lerow introduced the circular shuttle and so went into production with the first reasonably practical lock-stitch machine. This was seen and improved upon by a gentleman called Isaac Merrit Singer and so in 1851 was born Singer No. 1. The next five years saw a 'war' between the enterprising Americans who kept improving upon the basic design, and finally four companies pooled their patents and formed the Sewing Machine Combination.

At this time Singer had a partner called Clarke, who was a lawyer. He conceived the revolutionary idea of hiring out the costly machines whilst the purchaser paid in instalments. This totally new idea of hire purchase not only promoted sewing machine sales but had an enormous impact on the development of retailing far into the next century. Clarke's other original and ultimately far-reaching idea was to set up splendid showrooms to display and sell his sewing machines. In due course Singer also gave lessons and had a sample and educational workroom.

In the ten years from 1859 to 1869 the sewing machine trade became one of worldwide mass production. William Jones – who until now had specialized in steam engines – opened a sewing machine factory in Manchester; 1860 – New Home began in America; 1862 – Pfaff started production in Munich; 1864 – Frister Rossman opened in Berlin; 1869 – Singer began manufacturing in Glasgow and then in Clydebank.

What were these machines like? A French machine in 1860 had a slim and elegant free-arm! However, this idea seems to have been abandoned for nearly a century. The flat-bed machines were sometimes portable, sometimes fixed into quite sophisticated cabinets. They had a vertical needle, a take-up lever, presser foot and cloth feed. Vibrating shuttles and rotating hooks were gradually replaced by the oscillating hook developed in 1879. Both chain-stitch and lock-stitch models were available until the turn of the century and were often beautifully decorated with gilded flowers. Attachments were developed for tucking, ruffling, cording, braiding, hemming, quilting and free embroidery. Victorian fashions in dress and in household linens and draperies were far more elaborate than today and domestic machines far less comprehensive, and yet professional seamstresses and ordinary housewives all took great delight in practising amazingly skilful manoeuvres on their domestic machines.

With the advent of the First World War fashion had become very practical and anyway little finance was available for new sewing machine developments. Between the wars attention was directed mainly at innovations for trade machines but by the 1930s other large manufacturing companies of domestic machines had been formed: Viking Husqvarna, Necchi, Bernina, Vigorelli and Brother.

Although zig-zag stitching had been invented in 1882 and developed for extensive use in trade machines it was not until 1943 that Bernina manufactured their first portable, free-arm, zig-zag domestic machine. Suddenly machines changed dramatically: manufacturers vied with each other in the 1950s as they had in the 1850s to produce new ideas and capture the imagination of home sewers. Electric motors made control easier, lights were incorporated. Many features such as tension units and spool winders were built into the body of the machine for a more streamlined look. Brighter-coloured casings further changed the image.

In the 1960s Necchi were first with a single pattern selector, Elna were first with a range of ornamental stitches and Pfaff were the first with dual feed. The range of practical stitches and the embroidery developed at this time was extensive, and machine technology coped too with the sewing problems of synthetic fabrics. Completely new stitches were developed for the new materials. Forwards and backwards motion of the feed dog combined with side to side needle swing provided amazing stretch stitches for seaming, overlocking and embroidery purposes. Vigorelli developed an oscillating needle plate for zig-zag patterns of up to 12 mm wide and New Home developed machines with a 7 mm swing of the needle. Most machines provided variable needle positions allowing greater flexibility without the aid of attachments.

In the eighteenth century the industrial revolution touched the lives of everyone. Two hundred years later another revolution was to manifest itself: this time the electronics revolution came insidiously into our lives to bring changes of undreamed proportions. The mere touch of electronics in the sewing machine industry made incredible advances. Riccar were the innovators when in 1976 they used electronic components to give push-button control to dispense with the foot pedal. Various companies quickly incorporated the new technology mainly with the foot controls and with needle penetration. Thus slow stitch-by-stitch control was assured on all fabrics from flimsy voiles and silks to the heavy velvets, denims and leather.

Singer incorporated a microprocessor into a machine during the late seventies, giving instantaneous selection of stitches set to the exact width and length on the touch of a button. In 1980 New Home not only included a microprocessor for stitch selection but a memory bank to remember pattern sequences and exactly sized buttonholes. Styled 'the dream machine', it was exactly that: incorporating every possible technique and stitch for dressmaking and a calculated 630 million pattern combinations to embroider and embellish the fabrics.

Within four years six manufacturers were producing a selection of different computerized machines. New Home superseded Memory 7 with Memory Craft which possessed multi-memory capabilities; Viking were the first to supply a 'thinking' computer; Jones & Brother developed a *talking* machine; Frister Rossman's Logica was the most futuristically styled; the Pfaff Creative provided a digital readout sequence running over a display panel as work progressed.

The wizardry of computers projected our sewing into the space age. What on earth can possibly come next!

Glossary

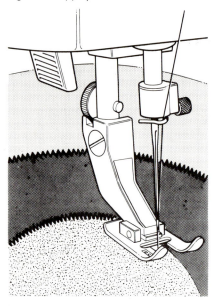

Figure 86 *Appliqué*

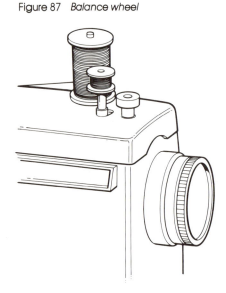

Figure 87 *Balance wheel*

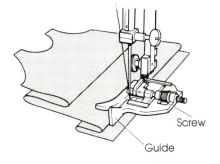

Figure 89 *Blind hem*

Appliqué A design from one fabric cut out and applied by stitches to another fabric. See Figure 86.

Asymmetric An uneven or out-of-proportion design.

Attachments General term for extra machine pieces, i.e. presser foot, quilting guide.

Automatic clutch Modern machines have an automatic clutch which disconnects when the bobbin winding mechanism is engaged. On older machines (and some of the basic or low-priced modern machines) the clutch is disconnected manually by the twisting of a plate inside the balance wheel.

Automatic lock On some computer machines the machine will sew several locking stitches on the spot and the machine will then stop sewing in the needle-up position. The threads can then be snipped off close to the stitches.

Automatic machine Most modern machines are 'automatic' – all the stitches (utility or embroidery) are produced by the machine with the aid of cams. When the particular stitch or design is selected the cam ensures the needle-swing movement is correctly altered during the sewing sequence.

Balance wheel Situated on the far right of the machine head, the wheel varies in size according to the model and make of machine. By manually turning the wheel the needle can be raised and lowered. The balance wheel should always be turned forwards – never backwards – when the machine is threaded, otherwise extra loops of thread could cause the machine to jam. See Figure 87.

Ballpoint needle Developed for sewing the modern synthetic fabrics and jerseys, these needles have a slightly rounded point which will slide to one side or the other of the fibres in the fabric. Ballpoint needles will also eliminate some of the 'skipped-stitch' problems common with this type of fabric. See also scarfed needle. See Figure 88.

Figure 88 *Ballpoint needle*

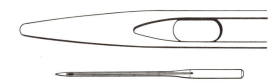

Bar tack The end stitches which are the full width of the buttonhole are termed bar tacks: they can also be used to reinforce the end of an opening or seam detail.

Basting Originally an American term for 'tacking', now universally used for machine tacking.

Batting Wadding used in quilting – American term.

Bias A true diagonal of 45 degrees across the warp and weft of the fabric.

Blind hem Type of hem where most of the stitches are on the turned-up piece of fabric and only an occasional stitch is on the right side of the garment. Dexterous handling can minimize the visibility of the stitch on the right side but it should be stressed that this is not an 'invisible' method of hemming. See Figure 89.

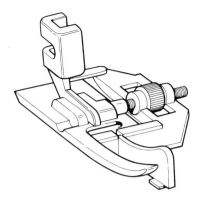

Figure 90 *Blind hem foot*

Figure 91 *Blind stitch hem guide*

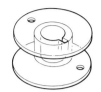

Figure 92 *Bobbin*

Blind hem foot Special presser foot supplied with the latest machines to assist with blind hemming. See Figure 90.

Blind hem guide Small metal guide inserted between the presser foot and the presser foot screw to assist with blind hemming. See Figure 91.

Figure 93 *Bobbin case*

Bobbin Small circular spool in plastic or metal inserted into the machine to hold the underneath thread. See Figure 92.

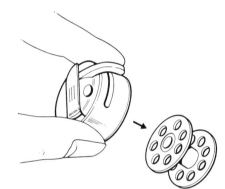

Figure 94 *Bobbin-winder tension*

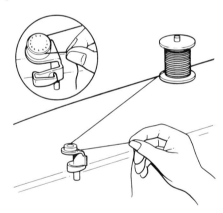

Figure 95 *Button sewing*

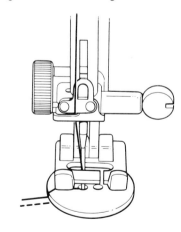

Bobbin case Small, metal, cylindrical case into which some bobbins are placed before insertion into the machine. There is an adjustable tension spring incorporated. See Figure 93.

Bobbin-winder tension In type these vary from model to model but always included on the machine is a small sprung disc through which the thread must pass between the cotton reel and bobbin during bobbin winding: if this is not done the thread on the bobbin will be loosely wound, uneven and cause problems during sewing. See Figure 94.

Braid Narrow trimming of various kinds used to embellish garments.

Butter muslin A type of muslin with a very open weave which was originally used in making butter. It is available from most good stores/shops supplying a variety of interfacings.

Button sewing It is unlikely that the sewing machine would be taken out just to sew on a button – however, when completing a garment it is useful to sew buttons in this way because unlike ready-to-wear garments the buttons are sewn with a lock stitch. Any zig-zag machine will sew on a button merely by dropping the feed dog. On some models an alternative needle plate is fitted when it is not possible to lower the feed dog.

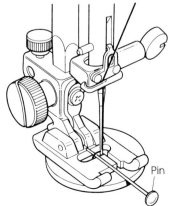

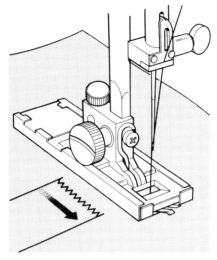

Figure 97 *Sliding buttonhole foot*

Figure 98 *Cam*

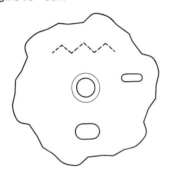

Figure 100 *Pattern cassette*

Buttonhole A slit in a garment through which to pass a button. Three types can be produced automatically on various modern machines. The normal straight-ended buttonhole can be produced on any basic zig-zag machine. See Figure 96.

Figure 96 *Straight-ended buttonhole*

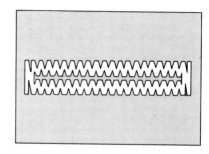

Buttonhole twist Heavy thread ideal for sewing on buttons but not normally for sewing machine buttonholes because the thread is too heavy and thick for this purpose. It is, however, a very useful thread for top stitching and embroidery work.

Cam Disc of metal, strengthened plastic or nylon with a shaped edge for variable motion of the needle in automatic stitching. See Figure 98.

Cassettes Interchangeable cassettes are available on some computer machines as a means of programming.

Figure 99 *Frister Rossman Guide cassette*

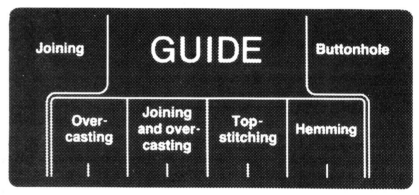

Chain looper A circular piece resembling a bobbin case to insert into the machine *instead* of the bobbin and/or bobbin case whilst sewing a chain stitch.

Figure 101 *Chain looper*

Chain stitch A line of stitching with one continuous thread which resembles a series of links. By its nature it will unravel when one end is pulled, making it useful as a tacking stitch. However, it can of course be fastened off and used for various decorative purposes.

Colour coding To assist with setting controls on semi-automatics, automatics and some computer machines the selector dials/knobs often have a system of colour coding. Thus the symbol of the pattern on the stitch selector will tie in with the same colour on the stitch-width control and the stitch-length control too. This helps the operator to ensure that stitches are easily set to the required standard.

Concealed (invisible) zip A specialist item easily inserted into garments in an invisible manner – when closed the zipper resembles a normal seam line. An extremely proficient method of closure – particularly on problem fabrics – ideal for all weights of fabrics and all types of garment. See Chapter 4.

Cord A fine rope or string which can be plain or decorative, inserted invisibly into fabric to give a corded edge, or it can be applied or couched on top of the fabric for decoration. *See also* piping.

Cording In sewing machine terms cording means to couch the cords in a decorative way on to the fabric – one or more cords can be used.

Correcting On computer machines the facility to review the sequence programmed by the user and to make corrections as necessary: this usually means cancelling out the program sequence *after* the mistaken letter or pattern. *See also* editing.

Couching A term used for a technique whereby a cord or thread of any thickness is laid on to the fabric and held there by a finer thread being sewn in a decorative manner over it. On a modern machine various stitches are suitable for this medium.

Cross stitch Thought to be the oldest embroidery stitch in the world and now available on the very latest computer machines. See Figure 106.

Darn To repair a worn or torn fabric by various stitches. Tricot stitch is one of the best automatic stitches for this purpose, but others are suitable. Automatic-darn sequences are contained on some computer machines.

Darning foot Free darning can be done in a similar way to free embroidery by moving the fabric around under the special darning foot. As the needle goes up and down the hook over the needle clamp causes the foot to rise and fall with the needle: thus the fabric is held tautly whilst the needle passes through the fabric but it is possible to move the fabric freely whilst the needle is out. This foot can also be used to do expert monograms.

De-clutch bobbin winding A modern system of bobbin winding whereby the bobbin on its winding peg is pushed into a locked position and the clutch is automatically freed. This ensures that the needle does not rise and fall during winding. Older models and more basic new machines require manual release of the clutch – by turning the inside disc on the balance wheel.

Digital display readout On computer machines a small 'window' displaying in numerical terms the stitch selection chosen by the operator.

Double-edged zig-zag A superb over-casting stitch on some computer machines.

Figure 106 *Double-edged zig-zag*

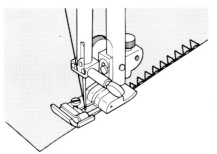

Figure 102 *Cording*

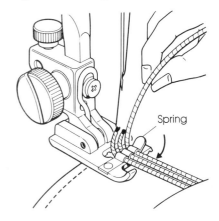

Figure 103 *Cross stitch*

Figure 104 *Automatic darn sequence*

Figure 105 *Darning foot*

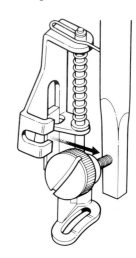

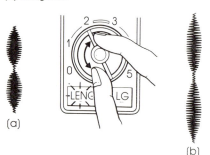

Figure 107 Elongated stitch length
(a) As programmed
(b) Elongated

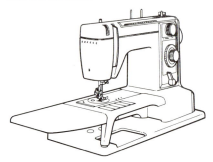

Figure 108 Extension plate fitted to a free-arm machine

Easy thread Most manufacturers now incorporate the easy threading system on their top machines. The system ensures that the thread slots into position through take-up lever, thread guides etc. and in fact does not need to be threaded through any holes until it reaches the needle eye. See Figure 8 and Chapter 4.

Editing On computer machines, the facility to review the sequence programmed into the machine by the user, and to make alterations without cancelling out all the sequence in so doing.

Electronic needle control This usually means that the needle is electronically controlled to always complete the sewing/stitch cycle and thus stop with the needle in the up position.

Elongated stitch length Some computer machines can be programmed to elongate a design without destroying the shape or the stitch density.

Extension plate/table Either a removable or additional sewing area around the needle plate and/or free arm. Most dressmakers successfully use the free-arm working area for all their work but when tackling larger articles a larger sewing area can be helpful. Extension plates can clip on, slide in, pull up, pull down, fold away, be built in or supplied separately!

Eyelet This facility is available on a limited number of domestic machines.

Faggotting A technique where two pieces of fabric are held together with a decorative stitch, such as a feather stitch, to provide an open-work seam.

Figure 109 Faggotting

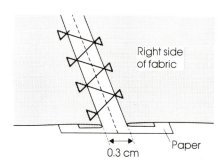

Figure 110 Feather stitch

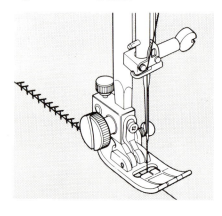

Feather stitch A hand-embroidery stitch which has transferred well to the sewing machine, with many decorative uses. It can also be very elastic and can be used as a utility stitch on stretch fabrics. See Figure 110.

Feed dog A small plate of parallel metal teeth which feeds the fabric through the machine and under the needle. It is altering the movement of the feed dog which does, in fact, alter the stitch length.

Felt disc A little red felt cushion which is placed over the thread spindle for the cotton reel to sit on to give smooth unravelling of the thread and eliminate – where possible – reel spin during sewing.

Flat-bed machine Traditionally shaped machine with a flat base plate.

Foot control The foot control/pedal will vary in size and shape dramatically from model to model but all have the same function: to control the speed of the stitching.

Figure 111 Flat-bed machine

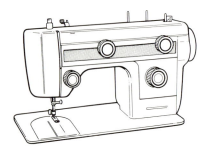

Free-arm machine Machine with an arm with adequate space around it to enable sleeves, trouser legs, armholes and suchlike to be positioned more easily under the needle.

Figure 112 *Free-arm machine*

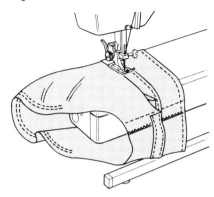

Free machine embroidery This is an art form in its own right and not the built-in embroidery stitches available by turning a dial, knob or lever on your machine. Free embroidery can be done on any machine at all – even a straight-stitch model – and it is necessary only to drop the feed dog and remove the presser foot, leaving the needle completely exposed. Some machines provide a special needle plate that fixes over the normal one instead of dropping the feed dog – but these are in the minority. The fabric must be supported by an embroidery hoop and then moved freely beneath the needle. The results can be incredibly artistic and in this way you may achieve monograms, pictures, etc. Combinations of embroidery and appliqué can be most effective. Free embroidery is not easy! Straight stitch and/or zig-zag may be used but much practice and perseverance are necessary. If you feel inclined to experiment it is recommended that a specialist book is purchased – there are a number on the market. The presser foot lever must be put *down* during sewing. See Figure 113.

Figure 113 *Free machine embroidery*

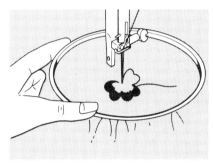

Gathering A process to reduce or control the fullness of fabrics by passing two lines of stitching through the fabric at maximum stitch length and then pulling up the bobbin threads (both rows together) to reduce the fabric to the required length. Gathers should be evenly distributed along the length and this is best achieved by 'stroking' the gathers with a pin!

Figure 114 *Gathering*

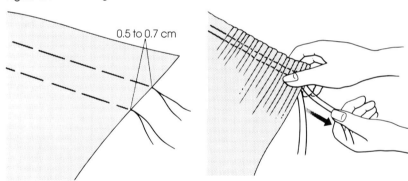

Zig-zag gathering As an alternative to shirring it is a soft and supple gathering for blouses, lingerie and children's clothes. Hold the elastic firmly in front and behind the presser foot and stretch the elastic – not the fabric. Sew a row of zig-zag stitches *over* the elastic, being careful not to catch the elastic with the needle. A shirring elastic can be used, or a fine cord/hat elastic, which is slightly stronger. See Figure 115.

Figure 115 *Zig-zag gathering*

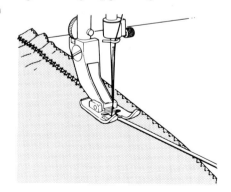

Alternatively, where a deeply gathered effect is required (i.e. rows and rows of closely spaced gathering), the zig-zag can be sewn over unstretched elastic and pulled up and knotted when sewing is completed.

Interfacing In dressmaking this is a medium placed between the outside fabric and facing to hold, mould, shape and/or support both stitches and the main fabric. It is most important to use interfacing and to be guided by the pattern instructions.

Interfacing can also be used to support stitchery on a fine fabric, i.e. embroidered motifs, buttonholes.

Interfacing is available in woven and non-woven mediums and is a very necessary aid and support to modern sewing.

Invisible zipper *See* concealed zip, and Chapter 4.

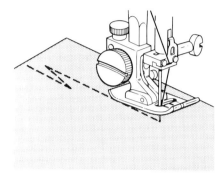

Figure 116   *Lock-a-matic*

LED   Light emitting diode. On electronic and computer machines the small (often red) light beside the selected pattern; or sometimes used as a warning light, i.e. bobbin running out.

Lingerie   From the French, we now use lingerie as an all-embracing term for ladies underwear and nightwear.

Lock stitch   All machines that use a top and bottom thread produce a lock stitch, i.e. the threads meet, twist and lock together with every stitch made.

Lock-a-matic   On computer machines a sequence where the machine is programmed to automatically sew a few reverse stitches at the beginning of the seam before forward sewing commences. See Figure 116.

Lurex   A metallic, untarnishable thread, which can be used by itself for embroidery or can be woven or knitted into fabrics.

Machine embroidery   Patterns/designs sewn automatically by the machine produced by means of cams or programmed by computer.

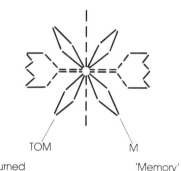

Figure 117   *Mirror image*

Manufacturer's handbook/manual   The instruction booklet that comes with the new sewing machine.

Mercerized cotton   Named after John Mercer who discovered the process to give cotton thread a silk-like sheen (in 1844). Sylko is the most famous but other companies use this process too.

Mirror image   Computer machines have the facility to turn over a pattern to provide a mirror image of themselves. See Figure 117.

Motif   (a)   In automatic-machine embroidery it refers to just *one* of the normal sequences used in isolation.
(b)   In general terms it can also refer to a small embroidered specimen piece which is then appliquéd on to the background fabric.

Needle   Long, thin, steel instrument with a point and eye at one end which when threaded passes through the fabric to create the stitches. Various types are available.

Figure 118   *Needle clamp*

Needle clamp   Holds the needle in position.

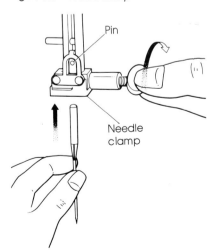

Needle plate   Plate that surrounds the feed dog; often graduated to show various widths of seam allowance. Some models need the plate exchanged for straight-stitch or zig-zag sewing. Machines that do not have the facility to drop the feed dog usually have a specialist needle plate or needle-plate cover to allow for free movement of fabric for darning or free embroidery.

Figure 119   *Needle plate*

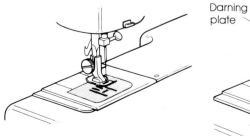
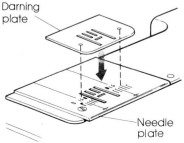

Figure 120 *Needle positions*

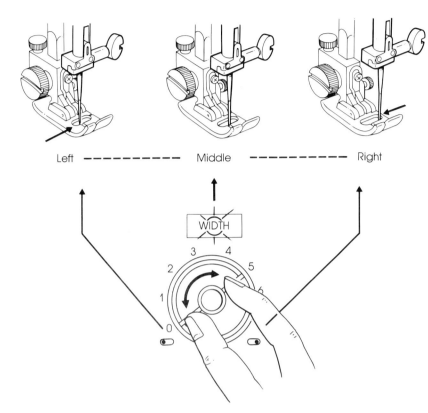

Figure 121 *Needle threader*

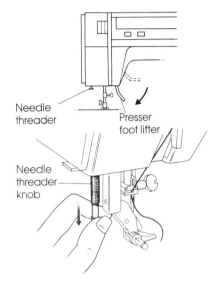

Figure 122 *Outline zig-zag*

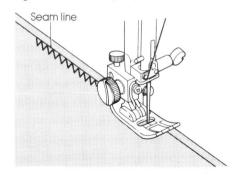

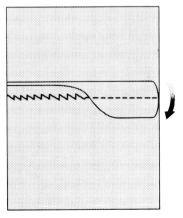

Needle positions   Refers to the position of the needle within the width of the presser foot during straight sewing. Some machines have one position only – some have left, middle and right needle positions. Electronic and computer machines can have anything from one to unlimited needle positions but the majority of makes have approximately twelve.

This facility is extremely useful to the dressmaker: it ensures that the fabric is held firmly and securely under the foot whilst the *needle* can be moved to sew exactly where the stitching is required, e.g. on the *very* edge of the seam/fabric or at a specifically graduated distance for top stitching.

Needle swing   The movement of the needle from side to side within the width of the presser foot.

Needle threader   A recent addition to the domestic sewing machine and now quite widely used by various manufacturers. A variety of types is used. They are usually set above and to the left of the needle and are pulled down into position whilst in use and then stowed away again when sewing is in progress. See Figure 121.

Needle up/down control   Normally a small button on the machine fascia on electronic or computer machines which is depressed to lower the needle into the fabric when required, i.e. turning a corner. This alleviates turning the balance wheel as on less sophisticated machines.

Outline zig-zag   A stretch stitch for bulked fabrics, i.e. plush, stretch towelling and Crimplene types. Unlike normal zig-zag the stitches give a Z-shaped effect because two small stitches are sewn side by side and then the fabric is pushed forwards and the machine stitches two more small stitches side by side. It is a very narrow stitch. When the seam is opened out this small degree of width is lost in the bulk of the fabric. A useful, firm and stretchy stitch for this type of fabric which gives excellent results.

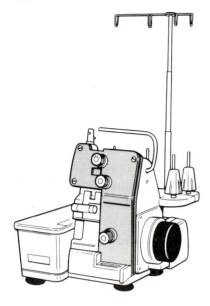

Figure 123 *Overlocker*

Overlock The use of two or more threads to encase a raw edge. Three threads provide a seam and seam neatening and overlockers with four or more threads are also available. It is usual to have the two seam allowances overlocked together to provide a narrow neatened seam 9–12 mm (⅜ – ½ in) wide and the overlock machine will trim off the surplus fabric to this width. See Chapter 8 and Figure 123.

Over-ride/manual adjuster On computer machines this allows the operator to over-ride the programmed settings of the machine and make his or her own fine adjustments or alterations to the stitches or stitch sequences.

Oversewing/overcasting Neatening a raw edge inside a garment – usually by zig-zag or a specialist stitch on the machine. See Chapter 3.

Patch-o-matic *See* pressure regulator.

Pattern An embroidery or fancy stitch.

Pin Modern pins are usually made of stainless steel – a fine wire with a point at one end and a knob at the other. Available in various lengths for different purposes. Glass-headed pins are extremely useful for dressmaking and craftwork and are long enough to sew over (at right angles to the stitching line).

Pin tuck A machine pin tuck is sewn with the twin needle. The bobbin-thread tension is tightened so that in sewing the two top threads pull together, thus creating a neat little tuck. This is very effective on a soft jersey fabric when rows and rows of tucks are the focal design feature.

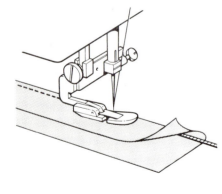

Figure 124 *Making piping*

Piping A fine cord enclosed in a bias-cut tube of fabric which is inserted for decorative purposes into a seam. Can be used in dressmaking, upholstery work or craftwork.

It is possible to purchase insertion-piping by the metre – this is a fine cord which is woven on to a 'self' strip of fabric: the strip is sewn into the seam allowing the cord to be exposed.

Plug Electric plug to attach to the mains electricity supply. *It is important to have the correct wiring and fuse.*

Figure 125 *Mains plug fitting*

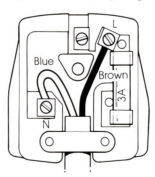

Important: The wires in this mains lead are coloured in accordance with the following code:
blue: neutral
brown: live

When leaving the sewing machine unattended, the mains switch of the machine must be switched off or the plug must be removed from the socket-outlet.

When servicing the sewing machine or when removing covers or changing lamps, the machine must be disconnected from the supply by removing the plug from the socket-outlet

Plush Plush is a fabric with a longer nap than that of velvet. Originally in the pure fibres – cotton, wool, silk – but now widely available as a stretch fabric in polyester and used extensively for leisurewear.

Presser foot The small foot that is fixed to the machine around the needle, which together with the feed dog holds the fabric whilst the machine is sewing: a variety of presser feet is provided with machines for producing various stitching techniques. *See also* under various specifications, e.g. zipper foot. See Figure 126.

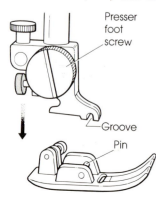

Figure 126 *A snap-on presser foot*

Presser foot lever The lever at the back of the machine, behind the needle, by which you raise and lower the presser foot. Some of the latest models have this lever to the right of the needle under the arch of the head of the machine so that it is easily moved with the right hand — it is indeed very practical when you get used to this new position. On the latest machines the lever can be raised to a second, higher, position to enable very thick fabric to be easily inserted under the foot.

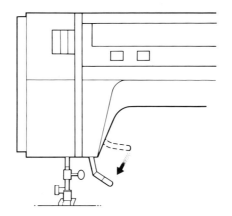

Figure 127 *Presser foot lever*

Figure 128 *Screw-on foot*

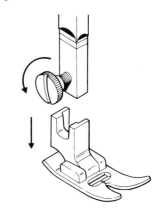

Presser foot screw On basic machines the screw holds the presser foot on to the machine. On more sophisticated models there is a unit on to which the presser foot can be clipped or snapped. This is a fast-exchange method for normal sewing; however, more intricate feet such as rufflers, still need to be fixed by the presser foot screw in the accepted manner and in these instances the clip-on foot unit needs to be removed. See Figure 128.

Pressure regulator An adjustable unit to determine the amount of pressure placed on to the feed dog by the presser foot. The pressure is extremely important in holding the fabric so that the feed dog can determine the stitch length accurately. Insufficient pressure may result in poor feeding, skipped stitches and difficulty in guiding the fabric. Too much pressure can damage the fabric.

Figure 129 *Pressure regulator dial*

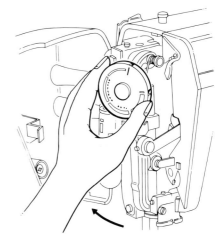

On the latest machines the dial to regulate the pressure is usually inside the face plate cover over the needle/light area; on older and basic machines it is usually an adjustable silver bolt-type regulator on top of the machines — this is sometimes called Patch-o-matic. See Figures 129 and 130.

Figure 130 *Patch-o-matic*

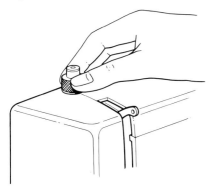

Figure 131 *Professional overlock*

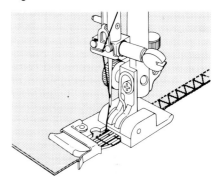

Professional overlock *Not* to be confused with the overlock done on an overlocker but a particular overlocking stitch available on one computer sewing machine. A very proficient overlock-type overcasting with a loop of locked stitches on the edge of the fabric. See Figure 131.

Program On a computer machine, a stitch sequence put into memory by the machine operator.

Figure 132 *Memory Craft programming buttons*

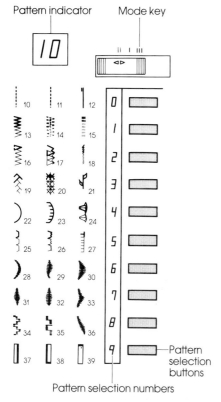

Programming buttons On computer machines, the control buttons by which the program is put into memory by the machine user.

PVC Polyvinylchloride. A fabric (often cotton) coated with a thick layer of a vinyl-based coating and normally used for rainwear and upholstery. Also used in leisurewear, camping equipment and craft items.

Quick-darn An automatic darning sequence in some computer machines. See Figure 104.

Quilting A technique to stitch together at least three layers of fabric to give a padded effect. Originally developed to provide warm, protective clothing, it can also be used purely decoratively. See Figure 133.

Figure 133 *Quilting*   Figure 134 *Quilting guide*

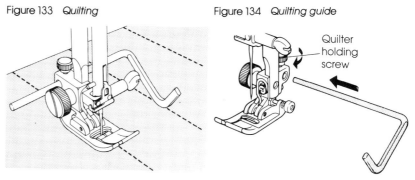

Quilting guide A curved metal bar which is attached to the sewing machine and serves as a guide to the consecutive rows of stitches in the quilting process. Quilting guides attach to machines in various ways – all are extremely simple. See Figure 134.

Ready-to-wear Factory-produced garments for the retail trade.

Reverse feed Backwards sewing.

Ric-rac stitch Is used on s-t-r-e-t-c-h fabrics in any area where a zig-zag would normally be used because it is a *stretch* zig-zag. It can also be used effectively for top stitching. See Figure 135.

Figure 135 *Ric-rac stitch*

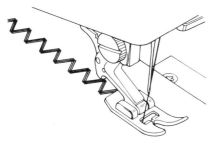

Roller foot A presser foot with small, scored rollers which will both grip and glide over problem fabrics such as PVC, leather, velvets and plush.

Ruching (ruffling) Whereas frills are usually gathered along one side to provide the fullness, in ruching and ruffling the fullness is usually a series of tiny pleats.

Ruffler A large presser foot which pushes the fabric to be ruched or ruffled into pleats of exact size: the size of the pleat can be altered according to the requirement of the machine operator.

Figure 136 *Roller foot*

Figure 137 *Ruffler*

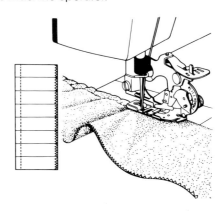

Saddle stitch Originally in hand sewing this was a stitch in a heavy thread to give a decorative finish to the edge of coats and other tailored garments. On the machine a very long straight stitch is usually used to try to copy this effect — the latest machines have developed various sequences of stitching (incorporating reverse stitches) to provide a decorative saddle stitch.

Satin stitch A zig-zag of any width but where the stitch length has been adjusted to allow the threads to lay closely together — side by side.

Scallop Derived from the shape of the shellfish, a scalloped edge is one of continuous semi-circles.

On some modern machines there are various stitch sequences to give a scalloped edge of various styles using satin stitching or open stitching or even straight-stitch sewing which can be adjusted to give large or very tiny scallops. See Figure 138.

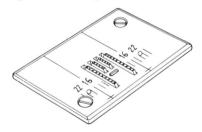

Figure 138 *Straight-stitch scallops*

Stitch length	Scallop variations
5	
3.5	
2.5	

Scarfed needle An improved type of ballpoint needle where the cut-away piece above the needle eye has been extended in length to that normally found. This needle was developed for jersey and polyester fabrics but will sew all light- to mediumweight fabrics very successfully including silk, cotton and lightweight wool. See Figure 88.

Seam guide (a) Guide lines scored or printed on to the needle plate.
(b) An adjustable attachment which fits beside the needle plate to determine the width of the seam allowance. See Figure 139.

Figure 139 *Seam guides on needle plate*

Semi-automatic machine A modified basic machine with a limited number of stitches and/or buttonhole which can be pre-set with a variety of controls — unlike the fully-automatic where the required stitch or pattern is dialled with a stitch selector.

Shell edging Usually used for lingerie or in babywear. A narrow hem is sewn with a straight stitch but periodically completely oversewn to draw the hem into a small shell-like shape — this is done with the blind hem stitch on the sewing machine. See Figure 140.

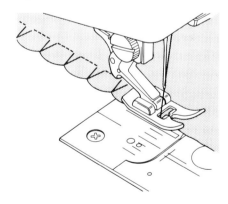

Figure 140 *Shell edging*

Shell tuck Used in lingerie, babywear and blouses it provides a dainty alternative to a straight tuck. It is sewn in the same manner as the shell edging.

Shirring Shirring in modern terms refers to rows of gathering with an elastic thread although it originally was a term to describe a piece gathered with rows and rows of stitches to give a ruffled effect. The modern elastic thread is wound on to the bobbin, rows of stitches are sewn and finally drawn up to the required size.

With the enormous scope of the modern sewing machine stitches and the latest developments in haberdashery there are now many acceptable (and easier!) alternatives to shirring that produce the same effect and are stronger in wear.

Shuttle hook Mechanism into which the bobbin fits. See Figure 141.

Side cutter Accessory with the Jones & Brother computer Galaxie which trims excessive fabric from the seam allowance whilst overcasting. Similar to an overlocker.

Sleeve arm See free-arm machine.

Figure 141 *Rotary shuttle hook*

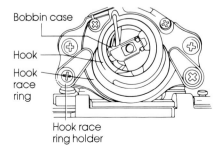

Figure 142 *Slide plate*

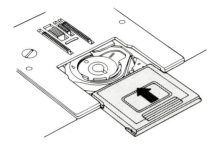

Figure 143 *Smocking*

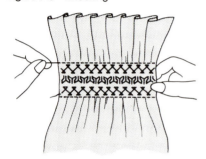

Figure 144 *Spool holder*

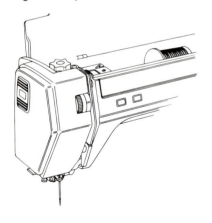

Slide plate   Sliding top cover to drop-in bobbin area. See Figure 142.

Smocking   A technique where after evenly spaced rows of gathers have been drawn up to the required size they are held in place with ornamental stitches. Machine smocking is not as regular as hand smocking but is most effective and very many of the machine embroidery stitches are suitable.

Speed control   Some models contain two speed settings for speed control: fast and slow. This can be on the head of the machine or on the foot pedal. It is advisable to use the machine normally on fast and get good control by use of the foot pedal as this is less likely to burn out the motor than constant heavy use whilst set at slow.

With *electronic* speed control there will be no loss of needle power even at very slow speeds.

Some of the latest machines have a slide speed control for effective accuracy.

Spool holder   Cotton-reel holder on top of the machine to hold the top thread – can be inside or outside the machine's head casing.

Stitch indicator   Panel of diagrammed stitches on the machine fascia beside which a movable needle/light (LED) or similar, indicates which automatic stitch has been selected and/or programmed. On a computer machine the stitch indicator could be a moving read-out in digital numbers.

Stitch-length control   Lever, knob or dial to manually adjust the length of the stitch.

Stitch modifier   A fine-tuner adjustment for altering stitch density on buttonholes, etc.

Stitch selector   A dial or lever on the machine fascia which is turned to select required automatic stitches. See Figure 146.

Stitch-width control   Lever, knob or dial to manually adjust the swing of the needle (i.e. the zig-zag width). See Figure 147.

Take-up lever   Lever above the needle through which the thread passes and which goes up and down during sewing, pulling the thread required for the stitching process off of the top reel of thread.

Figure 145 *Stitch indicator*

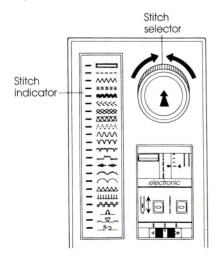

Figure 146 *Stitch selector*

Figure 147 *Stitch-width control*

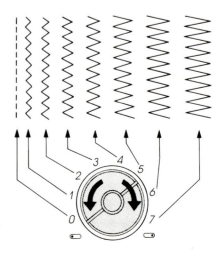

Teflon needle   A Teflon-coated needle developed for synthetic fabrics.

Tension   The tightness of the threads when making stitches is termed tension. There is a top adjustable unit through which the thread passes (which operates only when the presser foot is lowered). The bobbin usually has an adjustable screw to alter the underneath tension. In normal work only the top tension is altered *slightly* as necessary, however, tension rarely requires altering except when specialist threads or techniques are being used. See Figures 148 and 149.

Tension discs   Twin discs within the tension unit through which the thread *must* pass for the tension to be effective. Can be inside or outside the machine casing.

Thread (1)   All embracing term to cover a spun-out filament of yarn of cotton, silk, polyester, poly/cotton etc. etc.

Thread (2)   Passing through the thread (1) through the correct system – including tension unit – on the machine.

Thread cutter   Small sharp cutter to snick sewing threads. Older machines have a sharp area in the back of the needle bar, but the latest machines are incorporating extremely sharp and efficient cutters adjacent to the sewing area, on the base or in the casing beside the light on the head of the machine. Some models also provide another cutter beside the bobbin winder. See Figure 150.

Top stitch   In dressmaking a top stitch is a line of stitching to emphasize a seam line, or the edge of collar, cuffs, lapel or hemline. It can be a row of very long straight stitches, a special saddle stitch or similar or decorative stitches if suitable.

Tricot stitch (three-stitch zig-zag)   A zig-zag-shaped stitch with three stitches on each zig and zag! An effective stretch stitch. See Figure 151.

Figure 151   *Tricot stitch*

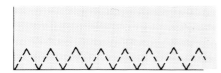

Triple needle   A three-pronged needle for decorative work.

Figure 152   *Triple needle*

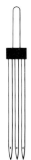

Triple stretch stitch   The true straight stretch stitch. It incorporates a reverse stitch every third stitch and is an effective straight seam line for heavier stretch fabrics. See Figure 153.

Figure 148   *Top-thread tension regulator dial*

Figure 149   *Bobbin tension*

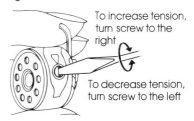

Figure 150   *Thread cutter*

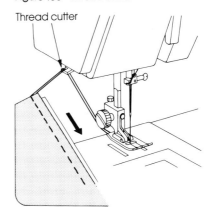

Figure 153   *Triple stretch stitch*

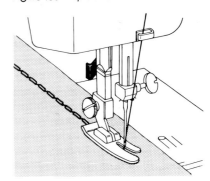

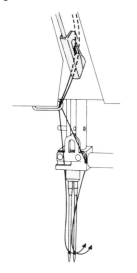

Figure 154 *Twin needle threading*

Twin needle   A two-pronged needle for decorative work.

Figure 155 *Twin-needle stitching*

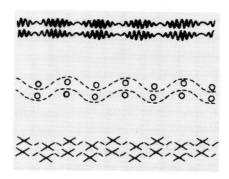

Utility stitch (working stitch)   A stitch used primarily for construction techniques, i.e. zig-zag, overcast, hemming, stretch stitch.

Velvet   A dense, short-piled fabric of cotton or manmade fibres. The pile can cause problems when it is sewn by machine because it tends to walk. Use a specialist foot such as a roller or even-feed foot.

Figure 156 *Twin-wing needle*

Wing needle   Needle that has two wings each side of the eye to enlarge the hole in the fabric during sewing. It is also possible to obtain a twin-wing needle. See Figure 156.

Working stitch   See utility stitch.

Zig-zag   A line of stitching where the needle swings from side to side taking a stitch each time. See Figure 157.

Zig-zag machine   A basic machine which will only sew straight stitch and zig-zag.

Zig-zag gathering   See gathering.

Zipper foot   A specialist foot for zipper insertion. There are a variety of different styles available but all do the same job. See Figure 158.

Note: invisible zippers need to be inserted with an invisible-zipper foot, not an ordinary zipper foot. See Chapter 4 and Figure 159.

Figure 157 *Zig-zag stitch*

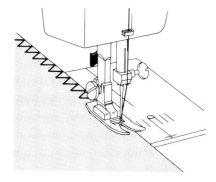

Figure 158 *Zip and zipper foot*

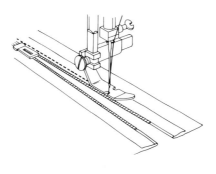

Figure 159 *Invisible zipper foot*

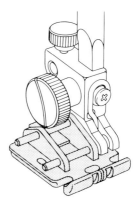

Index

accessories and attachments:
    blind hem guide, 26, 64
    chain looper, 66
    felt cushion/disc, 41, 68
    needle plate, 46
    quilting guide, 37, 68
    ruffler, 74
    seam guide, 75
    stowed in machine, 60
appliqué, 22, 24, 31, 33, 34, 64
asymetric, 64
automatic clutch, 64

balance wheel, 41, 64
batting, 64
bias, 64
bobbin, 34, 41, 54, 60, 64
    insertion, 41
    tension, 77
    threading, 17
    warning light, 54, 57, 60
    winder tension, 65
    winding, 13, 57, 58, 64, 67
braid, 65
butter muslin, 65
button sewing, 65

cams, 13, 66
cassettes, 54, 56, 57, 60, 66
clutch, 67
colour coding, 53, 66
computer:
    machine, 14, 51–61
    thinking, 58
cord, 67
couching, 67
craftwork, 15, 23, 33, 34, 37, 47, 53, 57

darn, 67
digital:
    read-out, 53, 67
    selection, 57, 67
dressmaking, 12, 15, 20, 23, 25, 26, 28, 29, 30, 32, 33, 34, 36, 38, 47, 48, 49, 54, 56, 57, 61, 69

editing, 5
electricity:
    mains plug, 72
electronic:
    foot control, 14
    machines, 14
    needle control, 68
    needle penetration, 14, 76
    pattern selection, 14
    speed control, 76
embroidery:
    free, 15, 69
    on leather, 35
    stitches, 13
extension plate, 68

fabric, 32, 33, 35, 36, 37, 45, 54, 56, 58, 72
    and thread, 37
    chart, 40
    difficult, 38, 47
    knits, 38, 47
    knitted, 37
    leather, 34, 38, 39, 47, 57
    plaids and stripes, 38
    PVC, 38, 47, 74
    silky jersey, 38, 47
    sportswear, 43
    stretch, 13
    upholstery, 15, 47
    various, 19, 35, 45, 47
    velvet, 24, 33, 38, 48
feed dog, 13, 68
foot control, 14, 16, 41, 53, 54, 56, 57, 69, 76
free arm, 12, 54, 75
free machine embroidery, 15, 69
fuse, 42

hand control, 56

interfacing, 69

jam, 41
jam-proof, 54

LED, 14, 53, 57, 58, 70
lingerie, 47, 48, 70

machine:
    basic, 12, 78
    choice of, 11
    cleanliness, 20, 50
    Combi, 50
    computer, 14, 36, 51–61
    electronic, 14, 36
    embroidery, 71
    flat bed, 11, 68
    free arm, 12, 69
    fully automatic, 13, 36, 49, 64
    getting to know, 16
    history of, 62, 63
    oiling, 50
    overlocking, 43, 72
    personal test, 14
    plug and electricity, 42, 72
    semi-automatic, 13, 75
    speed control, 76
mains electricity plug, 72
manufacturers' handbooks, 16, 19, 36, 46, 49, 70
memory, 55, 56, 57, 58
    corrector, 58, 67
    editing, 57, 60, 68
    override, 60, 72
    re-call, 58
microchip, 14, 51, 53
mirror image, 53, 60, 70
motif, 70

needle, 20, 32, 35, 41, 45, 46, 49, 71
    ballpoint, 35, 64
    care of, 35
    chart, 40
    clamp, 70
    electronic control, 68
    insertion, 35, 41
    jeans, 35
    leather, 34, 35
    penetration, 14, 53, 76
    plate, 70
    positions, 13, 54, 57, 58, 60, 70
    scarfed, 34, 35, 75
    size, 35
    swing, 70
    Teflon, 35, 76
    threader, 60, 70
    triple, 35, 37, 77
    twin, 35, 36, 54, 78
    up/down, 57, 60
    up/stop, 60
    wing, 37, 78

overlockers, 43, 44, 45, 46, 47, 48, 49, 50
override, 53

Patch-o-matic, 72
pattern sequences, 52, 53, 54, 55, 57, 58, 60, 72
    elongation, 57, 60, 68
    reduction, 57, 60
pin, 72
presser feet, 19, 46, 54, 56, 69
    blind hem, 19, 26, 48, 65
    buttonhole, 19, 54
    cording, 19
    craft, 19
    darning/monograming, 67
    elastic, 48
    even-feed, 34
    hemmer, 19
    lever, 73
    overedge, 19
    roller, 34, 74
    satin stitch, 19
    screw, 73
    snap-on/clip-on, 13, 54
    Teflon, 34
    zig-zag, 19
    zipper, 19, 78
pressure regulator, 73
problems, 20, 23, 35, 37, 38, 41, 42, 51, 56
program, 52, 53, 55, 56, 58, 60, 74
    buttons, 74
    sheet, 55

raceway, 38
ready-to-wear, 74
reverse feed, 74
rotary hook, 13

sensorized touch panel, 53, 57
shuttle hook, 12
side cutter, 56, 75
sleeve arm, 12, 69, 75
slide plate, 76
speed control, 56, 60, 76
spool holder, 76
stitch, 12, 19, 50, 51
   alphabet, 52, 55, 56, 57, 60
   basting, 13, 57, 58, 60, 64
   blind hem, 21, 26
   chain, 46, 57, 66
   control, 14, 54
   cross, 57, 60, 61, 67
   double chain, 47
   double-edged zig-zag, 25, 67
   double-edged overcast, 57, 60
   double tricot, 57
   embroidery, 13, 24, 31, 32, 33, 34, 35, 36, 53, 54, 56, 57
   feather, 19, 21, 24, 33, 68
   indicator, 76
   knit stitch, 25
   length, 13, 19, 46, 52, 53, 58, 76
   lock, 70
   modifier, 76
   numbers, 52, 55, 56, 57, 60
   overlock, 21, 25, 43, 45, 47, 50, 56, 57, 72
   professional overlock, 25, 73
   punctuation, 52, 60
   ric-rac, 21, 27, 74
   saddle, 57, 60, 75
   satin, 14, 75
   scallop, 75
   scrollwork, 57, 60
   selector, 13
   shading, 57
   straight, 11, 12, 13, 19, 21, 36, 54
   straight stretch, 21, 23, 24
   stretch, 13, 60, 70
   top, 21, 23, 77
   tricot, 21, 23, 36, 67, 77
   triple stretch, 21, 77
   utility, 13, 21, 22, 23, 24, 25, 26, 27, 31, 36, 53, 54, 57, 78
   width, 13, 19, 23, 46, 47, 52, 53, 58, 76
   zig-zag, 11, 12, 13, 19, 21, 22, 36, 54, 78

take-up lever, 76
techniques, 12, 13, 51, 56
   abutted seam, 47
   automatic buttonholes, 13, 28, 29, 50, 57, 58, 60
      keyhole, 66
      rounded, 57
   automatic lock-off, 57, 58, 60, 64, 70
   automatic quick-darn, 57, 60, 67, 74
   back-tack, 60
   blind hem, 26, 48, 56, 64
   buttonholes, 13, 54, 56, 66
   cording, 56, 67
   eyelet, 57, 60, 68
   faggotting, 68
   gathers, 33, 69
   hem stitching, 37
   patchwork, 35
   pin tucks, 36, 72
   piping, 21, 72
   quilting, 24, 34, 61, 74
   ruching and ruffling, 74
   shell tucks/edge, 25, 47, 75
   shirring, 75
   smocking, 31, 33, 76
   zippers, 29, 30, 56
tension, 20, 36, 54, 56, 58, 77
   discs, 77
   overlocker, 46
   units, 16, 17, 19, 77
thread, 17, 32, 33, 34, 35, 36, 37, 40, 41, 45, 77
   bold, 24, 32, 47, 56
   buttonhole twist, 23, 32, 47, 56, 66
   cops, 41, 47, 76
   embroidery, 33, 37
   guides, 42
   lurex, 33, 37, 47, 70
   mercerized cotton, 70
   overlockers, 47
   poly/cotton, 37
   polyester, 23, 32, 37, 56
   pure silk, 32, 37, 47
   spin, 41
   Sylko Supreme, 37, 47, 56
   unravelling, 41
thread cutter, 57, 77
threading, 16, 20, 36, 41, 77
   bobbin, 17, 18
   'easy thread' systems, 17, 18, 54, 68
   mis-threading, 41
   overlocker, 46
   twin-needle, 78

zig-zag, gathering, 69
zipper, 23, 29, 30, 33, 57, 67, 69